At Issue

| Cyberbullying

Other Books in the At Issue Series:

At Issue

I Cyberbullying

Louise I. Gerdes, Book Editor

GREENHAVEN PRESS
A part of Gale, Cengage Learning

GALE
CENGAGE Learning·

Detroit • New York • San Francisco • New Haven, Conn • Waterville, Maine • London

Elizabeth Des Chenes, *Managing Editor*

For more information, contact:
Greenhaven Press
27500 Drake Rd.
Farmington Hills, MI 48331-3535
Or you can visit our Internet site at gale.cengage.com

For product information and technology assistance, contact us at

Gale Customer Support, 1-800-877-4253
For permission to use material from this text or product, submit all requests online at www.cengage.com/permissions.

Further permissions questions can be e-mailed to permissionrequest@cengage.com.

Articles in Greenhaven Press anthologies are often edited for length to meet page requirements. In addition, original titles of these works are changed to clearly present the main thesis and to explicitly indicate the author's opinion. Every effort is made to ensure that Greenhaven Press accurately reflects the original intent of the authors. Every effort has been made to trace the owners of copyrighted material.

Cover image copyright © Images.com/Corbis.

LIBRARY OF CONGRESS CATALOGING-IN-PUBLICATION DATA

Cyberbullying / Louise I. Gerdes, book editor.
    p. cm. -- (At issue)
    Includes bibliographical references and index.
    ISBN 978-0-7377-5562-6 (hbk.) -- ISBN 978-0-7377-5563-3 (pbk.)
    1. Cyberbullying.. I. Gerdes, Louise I., 1953-
    HV6773.15.C92C93 2012
    302.34'3--dc23
                                       2011030421

Printed in the United States of America
2 3 4 5 6   15 14 13 12 11

FD356

Contents

Introduction

On October 17, 2006, in Dardenne Prairie, Missouri, 13-year-old Megan Meier hanged herself after receiving cruel messages from a boy she befriended on the social networking site MySpace. In reality, the messages were a hoax and came from Lori Drew, the mother of a friend of Megan. On September 22, 2010, Tyler Clementi, an 18-year-old freshman at Rutgers University, jumped to his death off the George Washington Bridge after his roommate, Dharun Ravi, and a fellow dorm mate, Molly Wei, used a hidden webcam to transmit images of Clementi having a gay encounter. On January 14, 2010, 15-year-old Phoebe Prince, who had recently moved to South Hadley, Massachusetts, from Ireland, hanged herself after high school classmates harassed her on Facebook, in text messages, and at school, calling her an "Irish whore" and "Irish slut."

These tragic deaths have drawn public attention to the problem of cyberbullying: the "willful and repeated harm inflicted through the use of computers, cell phones, and other electronic devices."[1] Criminal justice professors Sameer Hinduja and Justin W. Patchin, cofounders of the Cyberbullying Research Center, argue that cyberbullying has become a problem of epidemic proportions. Indeed, the Centers for Disease Control and Prevention in 2007 identified cyberbullying as an emerging public health problem. Pew Internet & American Life Project researchers discovered that one third of teens who use the Internet claimed that they had been threatened and harassed online and been victims of online rumors. Another study found that more than 70 percent of those who used the Internet and other communication technology regularly said that they had experienced at least one incident of online in-

1. Sameer Hinduja and Justin W. Patchin. *Bullying Beyond the Schoolyard.* Thousand Oaks, CA: Corwin, 2009.

timidation via e-mail, cell phone, chat rooms, or other electronic media. Suicide, however, has been a rare response to this type of bullying.

Nevertheless, experts have found strong links between bullying and suicide. Hinduja and Patchin maintain that bullying victims were nearly twice as likely to have attempted suicide compared to those who were not bullying victims. However, they caution, "it is unlikely that experience with cyberbullying by itself leads to youth suicide. Rather, it tends to exacerbate instability and hopelessness in the minds of adolescents already struggling with stressful life circumstances."[2] The circumstances surrounding the suicides of Megan Meier, Tyler Clementi, and Phoebe Prince were indeed complex. In a *Slate* article, "What Really Happened to Phoebe Prince?" journalist Emily Bazelon claims, "The whole story is a lot more complicated than anyone has publicly allowed for. The events that led to Phoebe's death show how hard it is for kids, parents, and schools to cope with bullying, especially when the victim is psychologically vulnerable."[3]

Following all three tragic deaths, the cyberbullies were charged criminally. A federal grand jury charged Lori Drew with criminally accessing MySpace and violating rules established to protect young people. Drew was later acquitted. The county prosecutor's office charged Dharun Ravi and Molly Wei with invasion of privacy. Ravi was also charged with bias intimidation, a hate crime, for targeting Clementi because he was gay. Wei was ordered to receive counseling and complete community service in exchange for cooperating with prosecutors. The case against Ravi is still pending. The district attorney charged the six students connected to the Phoebe Prince suicide with civil rights violations with bodily injury. The district attorney argued that Prince's civil rights were violated be-

2. Sameer Hinduja and Justin W. Patchin, "Bullying, Cyberbullying, and Suicide," *Archives of Suicide Research*, 2010.
3. Emily Bazelon, "What Really Happened to Phoebe Prince?" *Slate*, July 21, 2010.

cause she was called an "Irish slut," a denigration of her national origin that interfered with her right to an education. The bodily injury was her suicide. After pleading guilty, all six students were sentenced to probation and community service. Indeed, many Americans believe that treating cyberbullying as a crime is necessary to address the growing problem. Others believe that holding cyberbullies criminally responsible for suicides is unfair and will not effectively address the problem. Whether cyberbullying that results in suicide should be considered a crime is one of several controversies surrounding the issue, reflecting the complexity of the cyberbullying debate.

Those who oppose making cyberbullying a crime if it results in suicide argue that suicide results from many factors, including problems at home, clinical depression, drug and alcohol abuse, and alienation. Thus, they maintain, in most cases, cyberbullying is not the direct cause of suicide. The prevalence of teen suicide in general further complicates the problem. Suicide is the third leading cause of death for 15- to 24-year-olds. In a 2009 study, as many as 14 percent of US high school students claimed to have considered suicide. Adding to the complexity of the problem is teen brain physiology. Clemson University psychology professor Susan P. Limber claims that the brains of adolescents are not fully developed. Thus, she asserts, teens, unlike most adults, are ill equipped to comprehend the full consequences of their actions. "There is no question that some of the teenagers facing criminal charges treated Phoebe cruelly," claims Bazelon, who questions whether the teens charged in the suicide of Phoebe Prince could have anticipated the tragic impact of their cruelty. "Should we send teenagers to prison for being nasty to one another? Is it really fair to lay the burden of Phoebe's suicide on these kids?" she asks.

Cyberbullying experts such as Patchin believe that criminalizing cyberbullying will not adequately address the problem. Following the death of Tyler Clementi, he wrote, "the vast majority of cyberbullying incidents can and should be handled informally: with parent schools and others working together to address the problem before it rises to the level of a violation of criminal law." Even if evidence is clear that cyberbullying results in suicide, Patchin believes that that current laws are sufficient to punish offenders. "We certainly shouldn't pass a new law saying that if you cyberbully somebody and they commit suicide, you're going to get life without parole. That would be a mistake," he is quoted as saying in a 2010 article by Thomas J. Billitteri in *CQ Researcher*.[4]

Legal experts agree that cyberbullying that results in suicide is not a matter for the law. That a victim of cyberbullying might commit suicide is too unpredictable an outcome, these analysts assert. Paul Butler, a former federal prosecutor and now a law professor at George Washington University, argues in a *New York Times* article, "Bullies 'cause' suicide in the same way that a man 'causes' the suicide of a lover he spurns."[5] He explains that the law does not hold people accountable for results that they cannot predict. Moreover, he asserts, "Because suicide is a rare response to bullying, it would be difficult for a prosecutor to prove 'substantial risk' beyond a reasonable doubt." In order for an offender to be charged with a crime that they did not intend to commit, the prosecutor must prove that such actions would likely lead to the harm. Suicide, experts have shown, is not a likely outcome of cyberbullying. Moreover, Butler reasons, "When people are punished, it should be for the harm they intend to do. If a bully crosses the line between freedom of speech, invasion of privacy, or harassment, those are the crimes he should be charged with."

A majority of adult Americans polled about cyberbullying disagree. Of those responding to a 2010 poll, 69 percent believe that harassing someone over the Internet should be a

4. Justin Patchin, "Most Cases Aren't Criminal," in "Room for Debate: Cyberbullying and a Student's Suicide," *New York Times*, September 30, 2010.
5. Paul Butler, "Not Every Tragedy Should Lead to Prison," in "Room for Debate: Cyberbullying and a Student's Suicide," *New York Times*, September 30, 2010.

punishable crime. In fact, some *New York Times* readers criticized Butler harshly for comparing a spurned lover to a bullied child. One reader commented, "As a human in this society, you have no obligation to continue loving someone; you do have an obligation not to intentionally inflict harm." Still another Butler critic questioned the idea that punishment for a crime should always hinge on intent, citing laws that punish a driver criminally for killing others while driving drunk. In the same way, these commentators claim, cyberbullies should be held accountable for their irresponsible cruelty whether or not suicide was the expected result. They further argue that while programs to educate parents and teens about cyberbullying are important, the tragic loss of a young life should not go unpunished. Cyberbullying that leads to suicide should therefore be a crime, these commentators conclude.

The idea that those who use electronic media to bully others should be held criminally responsible if their victims take their own life remains a contentious one. When the court sentenced the six students charged criminally for the suicide of Phoebe Prince to probation and community service, commentators once again began to debate the issue. "What's the appropriate punishment for these kids?"[6] asks Vic Walczak, legal director of the American Civil Liberties Union, Pennsylvania. "I think these issues are going to be percolating in the courts for many years to come," he reasons. The divergent viewpoints in *At Issue: Cyberbullying* reflect the continuing debate about cyberbullying and its related issues.

6. Quoted in Thomas J. Billitteri, "Preventing Bullying," *CQ Researcher*, December 10, 2010

1

Cyberbullying Is a Serious, Widespread Problem

Jan Hoffman

Jan Hoffman writes on issues concerning teens, tweens, and family dynamics for the New York Times.

Cyberbullying, typically defined as repeated online harassment, is a growing problem among American schoolchildren. The unregulated anonymity of the Internet makes savage, psychological cruelty easy for cyberbullies. Indeed, the Internet erases inhibitions that might prevent adolescents from making vicious verbal attacks in person. Unfortunately, many parents, who are often not as technologically savvy as their children, are at a loss about how to deal with the problem. Moreover, some school officials believe they have no authority to intervene, and law enforcement officers require concrete evidence, which some parents do not know how to collect. Parents also struggle with how best to monitor online activity, trying to find a balance between giving their children online privacy and protecting them from Internet dangers.

Ninth grade was supposed to be a fresh start for Marie's son: new school, new children. Yet by last October [2009], he had become withdrawn. Marie prodded. And prodded again. Finally, he told her.

"The kids say I'm saying all these nasty things about them on Facebook," he said. "They don't believe me when I tell them I'm not on Facebook."

But apparently, he was.

Marie, a medical technologist and single mother who lives in Newburyport, Mass., searched Facebook. There she found what seemed to be her son's page: his name, a photo of him grinning while running—and, on his public wall, sneering comments about teenagers he scarcely knew.

Someone had forged his identity online and was bullying others in his name.

Students began to shun him. Furious and frightened, Marie contacted school officials. After expressing their concern, they told her they could do nothing. It was an off-campus matter.

But Marie was determined to find out who was making her son miserable and to get them to stop. In choosing that course, she would become a target herself. When she and her son learned who was behind the scheme, they would both feel the sharp sting of betrayal. Undeterred, she would insist that the culprits be punished.

[T]he Internet, its potential for casual, breathtaking cruelty, and its capacity to cloak a bully's identify all present slippery new challenges to this transitional generation of analog parents.

Slippery New Challenges

It is difficult enough to support one's child through a siege of schoolyard bullying. But the lawlessness of the Internet, its potential for casual, breathtaking cruelty, and its capacity to cloak a bully's identity all present slippery new challenges to this transitional generation of analog parents.

Desperate to protect their children, parents are floundering even as they scramble to catch up with the technological sophistication of the next generation.

Like Marie, many parents turn to schools, only to be rebuffed because officials think they do not have the authority to intercede. Others may call the police, who set high bars to investigate. Contacting Web site administrators or Internet service providers can be a daunting, protracted process.

When parents know the aggressor, some may contact that child's parent, stumbling through an evolving etiquette in the landscape of social awkwardness. Going forward, they struggle with when and how to supervise their adolescents' forays on the Internet.

[O]nline bullying can be more psychologically savage than schoolyard bullying.

Marie, who asked that her middle name and her own nickname for her son, D.C., be used to protect his identity, finally went to the police. The force's cybercrimes specialist, Inspector Brian Brunault, asked if she really wanted to pursue the matter.

"He said that once it was in the court system," Marie said, "they would have to prosecute. It could probably be someone we knew, like a friend of D.C.'s or a neighbor. Was I prepared for that?"

Marie's son urged her not to go ahead. But Marie was adamant. "I said yes."

One afternoon last spring, Parry Aftab, a lawyer and expert on cyberbullying, addressed seventh graders at George Washington Middle School in Ridgewood, N.J.

"How many of you have ever been cyberbullied?" she asked.

The hands crept up, first a scattering, then a thicket. Of 150 students, 68 raised their hands. They came forward to offer rough tales from social networking sites, instant messaging and texting. Ms. Aftab stopped them at the 20th example.

Then she asked: How many of your parents know how to help you?

A scant three or four hands went up.

The Vicious Side of Adolescence

Cyberbullying is often legally defined as repeated harassment online, although in popular use, it can describe even a sharp-elbowed, gratuitous swipe. Cyberbullies themselves resist easy categorization: the anonymity of the Internet gives cover not only to schoolyard-bully types but to victims themselves, who feel they can retaliate without getting caught.

But online bullying can be more psychologically savage than schoolyard bullying. The Internet erases inhibitions, with adolescents often going further with slights online than in person.

"It's not the swear words," Inspector Brunault said. "They all swear. It's how they gang up on one individual at a time. 'Go cut yourself.' Or 'you are sooo ugly'—but with 10 u's, 10 g's, 10 l's, like they're all screaming it at someone."

The cavalier meanness can be chilling. On a California teenage boy's Facebook wall, someone writes that his 9-year-old sister is "a fat bitch." About the proud Facebook photos posted by a 13-year-old New York girl, another girl comments: "hideous" and "this pic makes me throwup a lil." If she had to choose between the life of an animal and that of the girl in the photos, she continues, she would choose the animal's, because "yeah, at least they're worth something."

This is a dark, vicious side of adolescence, enabled and magnified by technology. Yet because so many horrified parents are bewildered by the technology, they think they are helpless to address the problems it engenders.

"I'm not seeing signs that parents are getting more savvy with technology," said Russell A. Sabella, former president of the American School Counselor Association. "They're not taking the time and effort to educate themselves, and as a result, they've made it another responsibility for schools. But schools didn't give the kids their cellphones."

Parents Looking for Help

As bullying, or at least conflict, becomes more prevalent in the digital world, parents are beginning to turn out for community lectures, offered by psychologists, technology experts and the police. One weekday night this fall, Meghan Quigley, a mother from Duxbury, Mass., was among the 100 or so parents who attended a panel featuring Elizabeth Englander, a psychologist who consulted on the new Massachusetts bullying law.

"I absolutely have to be much more techno savvy than I want to be," said Mrs. Quigley, who does not know how to text, although two of her children use cellphones just to text their friends. "But it is overwhelming to me."

[W]hile children may be nimble with technology, they lack the maturity to understand its consequences.

These lectures typically combine technology primers so elementary that elementary-school children might snicker, with advanced course work in 21st-century childrearing.

Dr. Englander reminded parents that while children may be nimble with technology, they lack the maturity to understand its consequences.

Then she demonstrated how to adjust Facebook privacy settings. Many parents peered at her slides, taking notes.

Don't set too much stock in those settings, she said: "'Privacy' is just a marketing term." A child's Facebook friend, she noted, could easily forward the "private" information.

In a study last year of 312 freshmen at Bridgewater State University, Dr. Englander found that 75 percent reported that during a typical high school day they had used their cellphones for voice communication 30 percent of the time or less, preferring to use them for texting, sending photos and videos, and surfing the Internet.

This is not a "phone," Dr. Englander told the parents who looked, collectively, shellshocked. What you've given your child "is a mobile computer."

If their children get caught in a crisis, she said, parents should preserve the evidence, by taking a screenshot of the offending material.

A mother timidly raised her hand. "How do I make a screenshot?"

The Bully Next Door

Throughout the fall, the Facebook profile set up in D.C.'s name taunted students: "At least I don't take pics of myself in the mirror like a homosexual midget," wrote "D.C." Also, "you smell weird." And "ur such a petaphile." At school, students would belligerently ask D.C. why he was picking fights on Facebook. He would eat lunch alone, and skipped some school, insisting that he was ill.

"I would always ask him, 'Are you having a good day?'" Marie said. "So he stopped talking to me about anything at school. He was afraid I would make more trouble for him. But the real victim was being ostracized more than the kids who were being bullied on his Facebook page."

She would call Inspector Brunault weekly. Last fall, the detective had to subpoena Facebook for the address of the computer linked to the forged profile. Then he had to subpoena Comcast, the Internet service provider, for the home address of the computer's owner.

Facebook has since made it simpler to report malicious activity. Although Facebook declined to make its head of security available for an interview, a spokesman replied by e-mail that if Facebook determines that a report of an impostor profile is legitimate, "We will provide a limited amount of data that helps the person take steps to repair his or her identity."

Finally, in January, Inspector Brunault told Marie he was getting close. He visited the home address supplied by Comcast. When he left, he had two more names and addresses.

A few weeks later, he called Marie.

Just before dinner, Marie broke the news to D.C. Two culprits were 14; one was 13. After learning the first two names, D.C. said: "Those guys have never liked me. I don't know why."

But the third boy had been a friend since preschool. His father was a sports coach of D.C.'s.

D.C. was silent. Then he teared up.

Finally, he said, "Do you mean to tell me, Mom, that they hate me so much that they would take the time to do this?"

Inspector Brunault asked the boys why they had done it. That summer, they replied, they had been reading Facebook profiles of people's dogs, which they found hilarious. They decided to make up a profile. They picked D.C. "because he was a loner and a follower."

Although the police did not release the boys' names because they are juveniles, word seeped through town. In the middle of the night, Marie received anonymous calls. "They told me my son should just suck it up," she recalled. "They said he would be a mama's boy. They would rant and then they would hang up." . . .

Should teenagers have the same expectation of privacy from parents in their online accounts that an earlier generation had with their little red diaries and keys?

Supervisor or Spy?

Should teenagers have the same expectation of privacy from parents in their online accounts that an earlier generation had with their little red diaries and keys?

Software programs that speak to parental fears are manifold. Parents can block Web sites, getting alerts when the child searches for them. They can also monitor cellphones: a program called Mobile Spy promises to let parents see all text messages, track G.P.S. [global positioning satellite] locations and record phone activity without the child knowing.

Parents who never believed they would resort to such tactics find themselves doing so.

Christine, . . . [a San Francisco] Bay Area mother whose daughter was sent links to pornography, struggled with how to supervise her daughter online. The challenge was compounded because students in the girl's grade were playing sexualized Truth or Dare games. Her daughter had a leading role.

Christine cut off her daughter's Internet access for months, mandating that she write schoolwork by hand. Over time, the girl earned back computer privileges. Christine also moved her to a parochial school. Then her daughter went on Facebook.

"We didn't know much about Facebook," said Christine, "but we set up serious monitoring." One program limited computer time; another blocked certain sites. Christine even had her daughter's Facebook password, so she could read the girl's private messages.

That was how Christine discovered 82 exchanges between her daughter, a freshman, and a popular senior boy at the school. Her daughter offered him oral sex if he promised not to tell friends. The boy wrote back, "Would it be O.K. if I tell friends but not the ones at school?"

Christine's daughter now sees a therapist. Christine herself uses a keystroke logger, software that records everything her two daughters write and see on their home computer. "It's uncomfortable," Christine said. "But my older daughter has demonstrated less than zero common sense. The level of trust between us is much lower than I'd like it to be. But I also think she was relieved that we caught her.

"My younger daughter calls me a stalker. She says we mistrust her because of what her sister did. That's true. But my eyes are open, and I won't go back."

Studies show that children tend to side with Christine's younger daughter. Last April [2010] in an omnibus review of studies addressing youth, privacy and reputation, a report by the Berkman Center for Internet and Society at Harvard noted that parents who checked their children's online communications were seen as "controlling, invasive and 'clueless.'" Young people, one study noted, had a notion of an online public viewership "that excludes the family."

Conversely, studies show that more parents are heading in Christine's direction. A recent study of teenagers and phones by the Pew Research Center Internet and American Life Project said that parents regard their children's phones as a "parenting tool." About two-thirds said they checked the content of their children's phones (whether teenagers pre-emptively delete texts is a different matter). Two-thirds of the parents said they took away phones as punishment. Almost half said they used phones to check on their child's whereabouts.

The Repercussions of Spying

Anne Collier, editor of NetFamilyNews.org, a parenting and technology news blog, noted that stealth monitoring may be warranted in rare cases, when a parent suspects a child is at serious risk, such as being contacted by an unknown adult.

But generally, she said, spying can have terrible repercussions:

"If you're monitoring your child secretly," Ms. Collier said, "what do you say to the kid when you find something untoward? Then the conversation turns into 'you invaded my privacy,' which is not what you intended to talk about."

Experts do not agree on guidelines about monitoring. But most concur on one principle:

"There is no one technology that will keep your kids safe," said Dr. Larry D. Rosen, a psychology professor at California State University, Dominguez Hills, who writes about raising a tech savvy generation. "The kids are smart enough to get around any technology you might use."

Dr. Englander installed keystroke logger software on her family computer. She uses it less as a monitoring device than as a means to teach her sons about digital safety. The Post-it on the family's computer reads: "Don't Forget That Mom Sees Everything You Do Online." She does not, in fact, check frequently. She just wants her boys to think before they hit the "send" button, so they understand that there is no privacy online, from her, or anyone.

Overburdened school administrators and, increasingly, police officers who unravel juvenile cybercrimes, say it is almost impossible for them to monitor regulations imposed on teenagers.

Last spring, the Essex County, Mass., district attorney's office sent the three boys who forged D.C.'s Facebook identity to a juvenile diversion program for first-time nonviolent offenders.

If the boys adhere to conditions for a year, they will not be prosecuted. According to a spokesman, those conditions include: a five-page paper on cyberbullying; letters of apology to D.C. and everyone they insulted in his name on Facebook; attending two Internet safety presentations; community service; no access to the Internet except to complete schoolwork. Their computers must be in a public family space, not the bedroom.

Marie, who reports that D.C. has a new circle of friends and good grades, is reasonably satisfied with the sentencing conditions.

But compliance is another matter. She believes that at least one boy is already back on Facebook.

Overburdened school administrators and, increasingly, police officers who unravel juvenile cybercrimes, say it is almost impossible for them to monitor regulations imposed on teenagers.

As with the boys who impersonated D.C. online, a district attorney's spokeswoman said, "That monitoring is up to the parents."

2

Traditional Forms of Bullying Remain a More Prevalent and Serious Problem

Susan M. Swearer

Susan M. Swearer, a professor of school psychology at the University of Nebraska, is co-author of Bullying Prevention and Intervention: Realistic Strategies for Schools *and co-director of the Bullying Research Network.*

To help bullying victims cope, policymakers should know the facts. Unfortunately, high-profile cyberbullying cases distract from more prevalent, traditional forms of bullying. In truth, as many as 25 percent of American schoolchildren continue to be bullied in traditional ways such as being hit, intimidated, and excluded. As few as 10 percent claim to have been cyberbullied. In addition, while most think of bullying as a schoolyard problem, bullying can also occur in the workplace. Policymakers should also know that prevention programs do little to reduce bullying. Programs that emphasize reporting and punishing bullies, however, have proven to be effective.

From schoolyards to workplaces and now to cyberspace as well, it seems that bullies are everywhere. New efforts to stop them and to help victims cope—such as the "It Gets Better" campaign—are gaining attention and popularity, but are they the best ways to protect kids and others from the worst forms of bullying? For them to have a fighting chance, let's first dispense with a few popular fallacies about getting picked on in America.

Myth 1: Most Bullying Now Happens Online

Cyber-bullying has received enormous attention since the 2006 suicide of Megan Meier, an eighth-grader who was bullied on MySpace. The suicide of Rutgers freshman Tyler Clementi—who jumped off the George Washington Bridge near Manhattan in September [2010] after his roommate streamed video of a sexual encounter between Clementi and another male student online—also grabbed headlines.

As tragic as they are, these high-profile [cyberbullying] cases should not distract from more traditional—and more prevalent—forms of bullying.

As tragic as they are, these high-profile cases should not distract from more traditional—and more prevalent—forms of bullying. Whether battling rumors about their sexual orientation, enduring criticism of their clothes or getting pushed around at recess, kids are bullied offline all the time. While it's hard to stereotype bullying behavior in every school in every town in America, experts agree that at least 25 percent of students across the nation are bullied in traditional ways: hit, shoved, kicked, gossiped about, intimidated or excluded from social groups.

In a recent survey of more than 40,000 U.S. high school students conducted by the Josephson Institute, which focuses on ethics, 47 percent said they were bullied in the past year. But, according to the 2007 book *Cyber Bullying*, as few as 10 percent of bullying victims are cyber-bullied. Meanwhile, a study of fifth, eighth and 11th graders in Colorado that same year found that they were more likely to be bullied verbally or physically than online.

[C]yber-bullying will be on the rise in coming years. But for now, traditional forms of bullying are more common.

Of course, with increased access to computers, cellphones, and wireless Internet—not to mention the exploding popularity of social media sites—cyber-bullying will be on the rise in the coming years. But for now, traditional forms of bullying are more common.

Myth 2: Bullies Are Bullies and Victims Are Victims

Actually, it is common for kids who are bullied at home by an older sibling or abused by a parent to become bullies themselves at school. Domestic violence and bullying feed each other. Researchers have found that elementary school bullies are more likely than non-bullies to have witnessed domestic violence during their preschool years. According to a 2007 study of bullying in Japan, South Africa and the United States, 72 percent of children who were physically abused by their parents became a bully, a victim of a bully or both.

But taking out their frustrations on kids at school doesn't help bullies. Researchers have found that bullies who are bullied themselves have higher rates of depression, anxiety, anger and low self-esteem than kids who are only bullies, only victims or who are not involved in bullying at all.

Myth 3: Bullying Ends When You Grow Up

Bullying is negative, mean, repetitive behavior that occurs in a relationship characterized by an imbalance of power. It can happen in a middle school—but it can also happen in an office. According to the *Journal of Management Studies*, nearly 50 percent of American workers have experienced or witnessed bullying in the workplace, even if they did not recognize it as such.

In that study, more than 400 workers in the United States completed an online survey about negative workplace behaviors. They were told that bullying occurs when an individual experiences "at least two negative acts, weekly or more often, for six or more months in situations where targets find it difficult to defend against and stop abuse." The workers reported verbal abuse (threatening, intimidating, critical and humiliating comments), physical abuse (throwing a paperweight, shoving, pushing, slapping) and sexual abuse (unwanted sexual advances and sexual assault).

Columnist Dan Savage's It Gets Better campaign is a worthy effort to convince bullied adolescents that their lives will improve. However, anti-bullying programs and legislation focused on schools should—and probably will at some point—extend to adults in the workplace. According to the sponsors of the Healthy Workplace Bill, 80 percent of workplace bullying is legal—and 72 percent of bullies outrank their targets.

Myth 4: Bullying Is a Major Cause of Suicide

According to the Centers for Disease Control and Prevention [CDC], suicide is the third-leading cause of death for 15- to 24-year-olds, behind traffic accidents and homicide. And while individuals who are bullied are at increased risk for self-harm, it's too simplistic to blame the deaths of victims solely on bullying.

According to the CDC, risk factors for suicide include a family history of suicide, depression or other mental illness, alcohol or drug abuse, a personal loss, easy access to firearms and medication, exposure to the suicidal behavior of others, and isolation. Bullying can be a trigger for suicide, but other underlying factors are usually involved. Interpreting a teenager's suicide as a reaction to bullying ignores the complex emotional problems that American youth face. To understand the complexity of suicidal behavior, we need to look beyond one factor.

Myth 5: We Can End Bullying

Can we? The debate rages on.

In 2008, a study of school bullying-prevention programs over nearly 25 years found that they changed attitudes and perceptions about bullying, but not bullying behavior. This isn't great news. Victims of bullying don't want to know more about bullying—they want it to stop.

Nonetheless, when schools collect data about bullying and intervene when they observe it, they can change the culture that supports the behavior. Programs such as Steps to Respect, Second Step, Bully-Proofing Your School, and the Olweus Bullying Prevention Program have proved particularly promising. A 2009 study in the *Journal of Educational Psychology* found that Steps to Respect—whose Web site says it "teaches elementary students to recognize, refuse, and report bullying, be assertive, and build friendships"—reduced bullying by 31 percent in some schools in Washington state. Parent training, increased playground supervision, effective disciplinary methods, home-and-school communication, classroom management, and the use of training videos have also been associated with reductions in bullying.

No program can end bullying in every community, and no program has eliminated 100 percent of bullying behaviors. However, when awareness of bullying becomes as much a part of school culture as reverence for athletics or glee club, we'll have a shot at finally stopping it.

3

Cyberbullying Has a Broader Impact than Traditional Bullying

Yalda T. Uhls

Yalda T. Uhls, a developmental psychology student at the University of California, Los Angeles (UCLA), conducts research with the Children's Digital Media Center. Psychology in Action, the website from which the following viewpoint is taken, is a project of UCLA psychology doctoral students whose goal is to communicate psychological research to those outside the field.

Significant differences between cyberbullying and traditional bullying make the impact of cyberbullying more severe. While victims of traditional bullying might feel safe at home, cyberbullying victims can be attacked from anywhere at any time. The audience for cyberbullying attacks is also much larger. Moreover, because electronic communication distances the cyberbully from the victim, the cyberbullies may not fully understand the impact of their behavior on their victims. While research shows higher rates of depression among cyberbullying victims, the results also show that cyberbullying is not as prevalent as traditional bullying. Nevertheless, cyberbullying victims and offenders alike agreed that the best solution was to prohibit access to social networking sites and take away computers and cell phones.

The suicide of a young girl named Phoebe Prince in January of 2010 received a great deal of media attention. Phoebe was the victim of bullying, manifested online by classmates who posted disparaging remarks about her on Facebook. A few months ago, digital bullying was again in the news when Tyler Clementi, an 18-year old college student, threw himself off a bridge [on September 22, 2010] after his roommate and a friend posted a webcam video of Tyler's sexual liaison with another man. Both of these deaths were featured in cover stories of *People* magazine, the second top consumer magazine in the United States (People.com). Because digital media tools allow bullying to happen beyond the schoolyards, twenty four hours a day, seven days a week, youth were using the tools to torment victims, who allegedly saw no choice for escape except to kill themselves. Journalists began writing about a bullying pandemic. Did technology unleash these forces, thus taking typical adolescent behavior and amplifying it to the point whereby drastic action needs to occur in order to address a pressing social problem?

[Cyberbullying] victims can be bullied anytime and from anywhere because most children have access to digital devices outside of school.

When one inputs teenage suicide into the search engine of *People* magazine, many articles come up beginning from 1978. One can also view a 1985 cover story about teen suicide with a picture of the then popular teenage actress Molly Ringwald entitled "Why are our children dying?." Indeed, teenage suicide has been portrayed as a serious issue, long before Internet access and use exploded. Nevertheless, the website suicide.org, which reports suicide rates, found that in 2003, rates grew for youth 15–24. This was the first increase in the suicide rate for young people since 1980. Perhaps cyber bullying contributed to this increase?

Comparing Cyberbullying and Traditional Bullying

Cyber bullying is defined as electronically mediated behaviors among peers such as making fun of, telling lies, spreading rumors, threats and sharing private information or pictures without permission to do so. One of the most consistently found differences between traditional bullying and cyber bullying is that victims can be bullied anytime and from anywhere because most children have access to digital devices outside of school. As such, it is difficult to escape this type of bullying, as long as one makes use of a mobile phone or computer. In addition, the Internet allows children access to a much larger community than in the past. Hence, a bully can torment a victim in front of a virtual audience of many people, such as a group of peers on a social networking site. The Internet also allows anonymity, and a bully can target a victim while shielded behind a computer screen or mobile phone. Finally, the asynchronous nature of electronically mediated communication allows for actions to be separated from consequences. In this manner, a person who bullies on a screen rather than face to face may not clearly understand how their behavior affects the victim. All of these unique aspects of cyber bullying may contribute to its potential effects.

Research scientists have begun to measure and disentangle where and how different kinds of bullying occur. Bullying is complex. First, several different kinds of bullying have been identified including physical and relational or social bullying. Second, prevalence rates change depending on frequency of the behavior. Third, separating out the location of the bullying is difficult as the overlap between victimization in and out of school is extensive. And finally, with respect to cyber bullying, different forms may lead to different effects.

Looking at Bullying Statistics

A recent study which separated different types of bullying was completed in 2005 in a survey of 7200 US 6–10th grade students; this study found that over a 2 month period, 13.3% of the students reported that they had bullied others at least once physically, 37.4% verbally, 27.2% socially, and 8.3% electronically. The prevalence rates for one time victimization in the last 2 months were 12.8% for physical, 36.5% for verbal, 41.0% for relational, and 9.8% for cyber forms. When asked about more frequent cyber bulling, defined as more than 2–3 times a month, 4.3% of the children reported being victims. Further analysis of the same dataset by the same research scientists found that the cyber bullying victims exhibited higher rates of depression regardless of frequency. Another study of US children completed in 2005 found that 13% reported being cyber bullied more than 4–6 times in the past year.

As might be expected, given that most schools do not allow unstructured access to technology during school hours, being a victim of cyber bullying occurs to a greater extent outside of school compared to inside school. In a recent study in Sweden, 16.2% of the children reported being a victim of cyber bullying outside of school, 9% in the school, while the total prevalence, % combining inside and outside of school, was 17.6, thus indicating a substantial overlap between the two. Most studies have found that the majority of victims of cyber bullying know the perpetrator, with many bullies being peers from school. The Swedish study separated the kinds of cyber bullying into text (email and text) and visual (video and phone). Text based cyber bullying was perceived to have a less severe impact than traditional bullying, but visual felt more severe than traditional bullying.

Examining Prevention Strategies

Given that peers from school are involved in most cyber bullying incidents, educators, compelled by legislation such as "Protecting Children in the 21st Century Act" are experimenting with different anti cyber bullying strategies. A recent study asked 713 middle and high school students which of 14 different cyber bullying prevention strategies would be the most effective in deterring bullies. The strategies ranged from curtailing an offender's access to computers both at home and school, to an offender doing a presentation about cyber bullying, to taking away the offender's extracurricular activities. The study also collected information on whether or not the student had been a cyber bully or victim in order to compare their perspectives of the most effective consequence. In fact, the top two perceived best strategies were the same for victims and offenders. These were "no access to social networking sites for the offender" and "parents taking away the offender's computers and cell phones." It's interesting to note that both of these strategies require parents to commit to the discipline of their children with respect to online behavior.

[I]n certain forms, [cyberbullying] does seem to have more impact that other forms of bullying and can lead to a significant increase in depression for victims.

Cyber bullying does seem to be a new challenge for youth. The good news is that it does not appear to be highly prevalent among youth, especially after one takes into account the frequency of the bullying behavior. The bad news is, in certain forms, it does seem to have more impact than other forms of bullying and can lead to a significant increase in depression for victims. One can speculate as to why cyber bullying may feel more distressing to victims. The larger audience, the around the clock availability of digital media, and the ease of dispersing embarrassing photos or videos, all of these affordances may contribute to a larger and more severe impact of cyber bullying over traditional bullying. The issue is still of great concern and research continues, as a cover story of last Sunday's [December 4, 2010] *NY Times* entitled "As Bullies Go Digital, Parents Play Catch Up" suggests.

4

A Lack of Compassion Has Led to an Epidemic of Cyberbullying

Ronald Alexander

Ronald Alexander, a marriage and family therapist, is a leadership consultant and the author of Wise Mind, Open Mind. *He is also the executive director of the OpenMind Training Institute in Santa Monica, California, where he combines ancient wisdom teachings with psychology.*

One explanation for the cyberbullying epidemic is a lack of empathy and compassion. Even compassionate children and teens may give in to the power of group thinking and participate in emotionally hurtful activities, particularly if they have experienced a significant change in their lives such as divorce or a recent move. Another explanation is Internet anonymity. The Internet, which can depersonalize those who use it, makes it much easier for those who are not taught empathy and compassion to make cowardly attacks on others from a distance. Although openness and freedom of speech are important, words can cause great psychological harm. Thus, parents and other adults in children's lives should act as role models for empathy and compassion.

We've all heard the horror stories of young adults and children having hurtful or embarrassing photos, videos and/or speech about them posted on the Internet for the world to see. But did you know that cyber-bullying can be as simple as sending an e-mail to someone who has indicated they do not want to have any further contact with you? I also have a personal dislike for all the chain e-mails that go out, especially those that indicate that something will or won't happen if you don't forward it on to 10 or more of your friends.

Explaining an Epidemic

Why are we experiencing this almost *epidemic* of malicious behavior? One reason may be a lack of empathy and compassion, which are both a behavior and an attitude. As a behavior, it is the capacity to place oneself in another's shoes and feel or relate to what they are experiencing. Empathy as an attitude is keeping one's mind and heart open to feelings, ideas, and concepts that may differ from what you yourself hold to be true. Compassion is a presence of being where one holds wisdom, understanding, love, appreciation, and respect for all beings in his or her own heart. The Buddha and other spiritual leaders teach us that we must even feel and radiate compassion for our enemies.

[A]nonymity can encourage kids and adults to be crueler online than they would be face to face.

Another factor is that anonymity can encourage kids and adults to be cruder online than they would be face to face. Even though the Internet is an extraordinarily valuable tool for our time, it also tends to *depersonalize* the people using it; this is especially true for those who already lack empathy. This aspect makes it much easier for cowards to throw jabs and hurtful words and become vicious with someone from a distance. For example, I seriously doubt that either of the two Rutgers students who posted the embarrassing video footage of their fellow student, Tyler Clementi, on the Internet realized that their lack of empathy and compassion for his sexuality would cause Tyler so much shame and humiliation that he would take his life by jumping off the George Washington Bridge. Tyler was a lovely, sweet and talented young man who harmed no one in his choice to be a gay American college student. Perhaps had these students been taught empathy, compassion and mindfulness at home, church, mosque, temple or school, this terrible tragedy could have been averted?

A Poor Use of Energy

Sites like Facebook, Twitter and MySpace need openness, but freedom of speech should also take into consideration that words can be powerful weapons and if not used mindfully can inflict deep and hurtful psychological wounds. Inflicting injuries from a distance is in itself a cruel and inhuman manner to respond to another being's feelings and sense of self. From both a Zen and a psychological view, if you have an unwholesome intention and are consciously choosing to attack others, you are limiting your own capacity for change and stunting the creative unfolding of your own life. Your energy is being wasted on the futile effort of trying to force the external world to conform to your vision. The mental and emotional effort required to maintain this negative energy and pretense is enormous. Having wise intention is more than merely being ethical; it's necessary for one's psychological well-being and clear thinking.

Then there are those, especially children and teenagers, who may normally have a strong sense of self and compassion but find themselves giving in to "group thinking" and becoming emotionally hurtful. For various reasons they can become swept up into activities that are incongruous with the values and behaviors they were taught. Divorce, a change in family dynamics or friends and even moving to a new neighborhood can stir up deep unconscious feelings of resentment, hurt, loss and abandonment. Often simmering on the surface of these feelings is anger. Acting out this anger is easier than struggling with the deeper issues that require awareness and mindfulness of the sorrow, loss and vulnerability children feel when sudden and shocking changes occur. It is not good enough to simply teach your children strong values and codes of wise and right conduct, but one should also discuss with them how to handle those moments when they are pressured by their peers or predatory adults. Several of the children I grew up with in the 60s ended up in spiritual cults, one of which was in the top 10 percent of my high school graduating class. He was bullied spiritually into submission by a cult leader guru who caused him enormous pain and suffering.

[W]e can imagine and grow an entirely new cyber-generation of mindful, compassionate beings who are more tolerant....

Mirroring Compassion and Empathy

So how can we eradicate this malevolent behavior? Gandhi said you must be the change you desire. This starts with coaches, teachers, parents and others who need to mirror compassion and empathy along with understanding and care in all situations, even in the most extreme of life expectancies.

I think it would be great to create a bumper sticker that says, "It's Not Cool To Be Cruel!" I council my patients to talk with their children and teens at home over dinner, in the car and in the family living room on how to be more courageous, empathic and compassionate. It is important for them to understand the destructive nature of cruelty and how it can destroy lives. They also need to learn how the values of creativity and hope can inspire and help people feel that growth is possible. This way they can discover that contributing to another being's growth and transformation is far superior to tearing down or taking apart their sense of self. Of course the best way for children to learn this lesson is to see it in action through their role models and parents. All the best heartfelt discussions can fall on deaf ears if the caring adults are unable to set an example and "walk their talk."

As Crosby, Stills, Nash and Young sang, "Teach your children well." From this great lyric we can imagine and grow an entirely new cyber-generation of mindful, compassionate beings who are more tolerant of all races, colors, creeds and sexual orientations. We can all live in peace. So let's all join together and become more mindful *now!*

5

Increased Access to Electronic Media Fosters Cyberbullying

Jennifer Holladay

Jennifer Holladay, former senior adviser for strategic affairs at the Southern Poverty Law Center and former director of its Teaching Tolerance Project, lectures and writes on issues of difference.

Nearly all children have access to electronic media. Indeed, 2010 research shows that 93 percent of children have computers at home and 66 percent have cell phones. Cyberbullies use this electronic technology to repeatedly harass, humiliate, or threaten their victims. Moreover, unlike traditional bullies, cyberbullies deliver their hateful messages in front of a much larger audience. Surprisingly, when parents learn that their children are cyberbullying victims or offenders, they claim to be unaware of their children's online activity. Programs to address the problem should help parents teach more than online safety. They should help develop empathy and clarify misconceptions about Internet anonymity. Children should also know that what they post on the Internet is permanent.

The stakes have never been higher for students—or schools. Phoebe Prince is loved by her peers. At least, now she is.

A Bullicide in South Hadley

Hundreds of people have lent their voices to support her on Facebook. Taylor Gosselin wrote, "Your story touched my heart." Dori Fitzgerald Acevedo added, "I am so glad we are not letting this get swept under the carpet."

Jennifer Holladay, "Cyberbullying: The Stakes Have Never Been Higher for Students—or Schools," *Teaching Tolerance*, Fall 2010, pp. 42–45. www.tolerance.org. Copyright © 2010 by Southern Poverty Law Center. Reproduced by permission.

"This" is what some might call bullicide—suicide by bullying.

Before Phoebe Prince hanged herself, she was a new student at South Hadley High School in South Hadley, Massachusetts. Phoebe was a newly arrived Irish immigrant, but that doesn't seem to be what ignited the ire of her peers—or her own self-doubt. Instead, Phoebe reportedly dared to date boys whom others thought should be off limits to her.

Girls at Phoebe's school reportedly called her an "Irish slut," a "whore" and a "bitch," viciously harassing her in person and on Facebook. Public documents indicate that at least one student gloated after Phoebe took her own life, "I don't care that she's dead."

Phoebe's tormentors have since been dubbed the "Mean Girls," after the clique in the 2004 Tina Fey-scripted movie of the same name. And for the Mean Girls of South Hadley, the consequences of their purported actions have been severe. They are now maligned across the Internet, from postings on Facebook to the comment areas of news websites worldwide.

The Mean Girls, along with two male students, also face an array of criminal charges for allegedly bullying Phoebe Prince. Since then, it's become clear that Phoebe's reasons for taking her own life were complicated. She had struggled with depression and had even attempted suicide once before. But the bullying she endured definitely had an impact on her.

New Term, Old Concept

Cyberbullying. The word didn't even exist a decade ago, yet the problem is pervasive in children's lives today.

Simply put, cyberbullying is the repeated use of technology to harass, humiliate or threaten. When fingers take to the keyboard, or thumbs type into a cell phone and craft messages of hate or malice about a specific person, cyberbullying is emerging. And unlike most types of traditional bullying, it comes with a wide audience.

"You can pass around a note to classmates making fun of a peer, and it stays in the room," said Sheri Bauman, a 30-year education veteran who now works as director of the school counseling master's degree program at the University of Arizona. "But when you post that same note online, thousands can see it. The whole world becomes witness and is invited to participate."

"Wherever kids go with their computers or phones, which is nearly everywhere, the bullies come with them."

The Suicide Connection

Anywhere from one-third to one-half of youths have been targeted by cyberbullies. And those experiences produce damaging consequences—everything from a decline in academic performance to thoughts about suicide.

"Our study of upwards of 2,000 middle school students revealed that cyberbullying victims were nearly twice as likely to attempt suicide compared to students not targeted with online abuse," said Sameer Hinduja, the study co-author, who is also an associate professor at Florida Atlantic University and a founder of the Cyberbullying Research Center. "Cyberbullying clearly heightens instability and hopelessness in adolescents' minds."

Findings like these, and actual deaths like Phoebe's, lend a sense of urgency to anti-cyberbullying efforts. Legally speaking, those efforts can be tricky for school administrators. The judiciary has long struggled to balance freedom of speech against the darker side of digital communication.

More and more though, courts and law enforcement are sending the message that cyberbullying will not be tolerated. For instance, in March 2010, California's Second Appellate District concluded that online threats against a student were not protected speech and allowed a civil lawsuit against the alleged perpetrators, their parents and school officials to proceed.

Today, 93 percent of children ages 8 to 18 have computers at home. . . .

A Tall Order

The notion that schools must respond to behavior that takes place off-campus and online may seem like a tall order. But schools are coming to understand that bullies don't just attack in the cafeteria or on the playground. "Wherever kids go with their computers or phones, which is nearly everywhere, the bullies come with them," explained Bauman.

A 2010 study by the Henry J. Kaiser Family Foundation found that technology access among children has skyrocketed since 1999. Today, 93 percent of children ages 8 to 18 have computers at home, 66 percent have personal cell phones (on which they are more likely to text than talk), and 76 percent own another multimedia device, such as an iPod.

These tools give them access to a dizzying array of social media. Some of them, such as Twitter and Facebook, are well known among parents and teachers. But others, such as Formspring, fly well below the radar of most adults. Yet it's sites like Formspring that can create the biggest headaches. Formspring offers its users total anonymity. That makes it at once a huge draw for curious teenagers and a nearly perfect medium for cyberbullies.

Relieving the Drama

The ostensible boundary between off-campus behavior and school life evaporated for Highline Academy, a K-8 charter in Denver, last spring when a conflict fueled by Facebook posts ultimately led to a physical altercation in the middle school.

"When I looked at the pages, I was shocked by how freely and harshly the kids were talking to and about one another," said principal Gregg Gonzales.

In the wake of the incident, Highline officials spoke with students in morning meetings and issued a special packet of information to parents and guardians about cyberbullying and Internet safety. Still, a new Facebook page soon appeared, with a growing stream of posts about a student directly involved in the altercation.

"As a community, we needed to step back from the incident and relieve some of the drama," Gonzales said. He asked every parent in the middle school to support a 48-hour moratorium on Facebook activity at home. He also asked parents to discuss the use of the social networking site with their children.

[P]arents nationally underestimate children's use of social networking sites and often are unaware of how, they are used.

Gonzales and his colleagues also placed personal phone calls to parents of students who had engaged in the online conversations. "It may be outside our jurisdiction to dictate what students do on their own time, but it was important to let parents know we'd discovered their child had engaged in cyberbullying or inappropriate conversations about the incident," Gonzales said.

As it turned out, his initial shock about students' online behavior was shared. "Numerous parents came back to us and said, 'I had no idea'—no idea what their child was doing online, or even that they had a Facebook page."

Such responses are typical. A 2009 study from Common Sense Media found that parents nationally underestimate children's use of social networking sites and often are unaware of *how* they are used. Thirty-seven percent of students, for example, admitted they'd made fun of a peer online, but only 18 percent of parents thought their child would engage in such conduct.

"The episode taught us—teachers, parents and students—that practicing respect, one of our core values, means practicing it wherever we are, at school or online," Gonzales said.

Getting in Front of the Problems

The Seattle Public School District took a proactive stance last year when it launched a pilot curriculum to prevent cyberbullying in its junior high and middle schools.

Mike Donlin, the senior program consultant who led the curriculum's development, says the district chose to create its own resources rather than use off-the-shelf products. This ensured that the resources would be easy to use and easy to integrate into existing curricula. "There also was the issue of cost," he said. "We believed we could create something great with far less expense."

Unlike many programs that address cyberbullying piecemeal—focusing only on Internet safety skills, for example—the Seattle curriculum attacked the entire problem. It did this by using the four most promising prevention practices. They are:

- Debunking misperceptions about digital behavior;

- Building empathy and understanding;

- Teaching online safety skills;

- Equiping young people with strategies to reject digital abuse in their lives.

The Seattle curriculum also recognizes the importance of parental engagement by offering take-home letters and activities.

Academically, the curriculum focuses on writing. This not only boosts student skills in a tested area, it also allows the program to discard common, ineffective practices. Instead of asking students to sign a pre-crafted pledge, for example, the curriculum prompts children to write personal contracts for themselves about their online behavior.

The curriculum also educates teachers about cyberbullying and introduces a language they can share with their students. "We couch lessons in a way that resonates for teachers, too," said Donlin. "So, we use the Golden Rule. We use the old-fashioned mantra 'don't kiss and tell' to address sexting."

Shifting Roles

Still, some information requires repeated explanation. Some might wonder, for example, why the curriculum prompts students to try to see things from the *bully's* perspective. "A single student can be a victim, a bystander and a bully in different moments," Donlin explained. "Maybe a child was bullied at school this morning, but gets online later and bullies back. Their roles shift. Technology gives them tremendous freedom and power to reach out and touch in nearly every moment, for good or evil."

Learning how to resist the urge to "bully back" is important for many students, as is un-learning some common myths about being online. Kids often think they can be anonymous on the Internet, or that what they do there is fleeting. Both ideas are mistaken. The Library of Congress, for example, is archiving all Twitter messages sent from March 2006 forward. Even the "mean tweets" will be immortalized for future generations. "Everything students do online reflects on them, permanently," says Donlin.

[C]yberbullying, like traditional bullying, is about power.

For teachers, a common stumbling block revolves around First Amendment protections and discomfort about corralling students' speech. Donlin believes that should not be a problem in most cases. "We have Second Amendment rights to possess weapons, but that doesn't mean we allow children to bring guns to school," he observed. "When it comes to cyberbullying, we're still talking about school safety."

The new curriculum hasn't been a total remedy for Seattle's schools. In January, one middle school suspended two dozen students who "friended" or became "fans" of a Facebook page maligning another child. It was a reminder that, despite the best efforts, a school's struggle against cyberbullying never ends. "Phoebe Prince was lost earlier this year," Donlin said. "There were others before her. . . . Their names and stories faded. My fear is that we'll forget the lesson learned—again. We have to teach this *now*."

Is Cyberbullying Largely a Problem for Girls?

Conventional wisdom suggests that boys are more likely to bully in person and girls are more likely to bully online. Sheri Bauman, the director of the school counseling master's degree program at the University of Arizona, cautions against jumping to conclusions. "Cyberbullying is a new area of inquiry, and it's just hard to draw definitive conclusions from the research that's currently available," she said.

What is clear is that cyberbullying, like traditional bullying, is about power. "Students attempt to gain social status through cyberbullying," said Bauman. Sameer Hinduja of the Cyberbullying Research Center says that gaining social status often means tearing someone else down, and *boys and girls often do that differently.*

"Girls tend to target each other with labels that carry particular meanings for them," said Hinduja. Labels like "slut," "whore" and "bitch" the epithets reportedly used against Phoebe Prince—are common within girl-to-girl cyberbullying. The main tactic of boy cyberbullies who attack other boys is to accuse them of being gay. "The amount of abuse boys encounter because of real or perceived sexual orientation is pronounced," Bauman said.

Disciplining Bullies

Advocates have spent years trying to get schools to take cyberbullying and its traditional counterpart seriously. It's no wonder then that so many express support for increasingly harsh consequences being handed out across the country.

When a prosecutor charged nine students with criminal offenses related to bullying Phoebe Prince, Elizabeth Englander, director of the Massachusetts Aggression Reduction Center, called it a "watershed" moment. Across the country, in Seattle, after more than 20 students were suspended for taunting a classmate online, Mike Donlin, a senior consultant in the district, called it "a clear message—hard and fast." Many states and districts mandate required punishments like suspension or expulsion, and some are now considering heftier use of criminal penalties as well.

Sheri Bauman, the director of the school counseling master's degree program at the University of Arizona, encourages everyone to take a deep breath.

"Pushing children out of school isn't going to help," she said. "Bullying, online and in person, is rarely solved with punitive methods. Children who are punished typically persist; they just change their methods."

Bauman, who has studied cyberbullying and its traditional counterpart in the United States, Australia, Canada, Germany and Norway, points to different models of justice. She prefers the "Method of Shared Concern," which involves all parties— the bully, the victim and the bystanders—in examining and addressing conflicts. However, this needs to be done by educators who have been properly trained or it can make the situation worse.

"We need to expand our toolbox," Bauman said. "Punishments may make us feel better or safer, but other options can yield actual results."

6

Cyberbullies and Victims Have Mental and Emotional Health Problems

Steven Reinberg

Steven Reinberg, a senior staff writer for HealthDay, *is an award-winning health journalist who has written for both consumer and professional audiences. His work has also appeared in* Reuters Health *and* The Scientist.

Studies show that both victims and their cyberbullies suffer from mental, behavioral, and emotional health problems. Victims often come from broken homes and find it hard to get along with others. Cyberbullies are more prone to hyperactivity and conduct problems and often smoke and drink. Both cyberbullies and their victims report feeling unsafe at school. However, victims have a more generalized fear for their safety as cyberbullying can occur anywhere, at any time. Since the impact of cyberbullying is often felt at school, schools have become more active in developing anti-bullying programs. With as many as one-third of teens in the United States report being victims of bullying, parents and communities must also respond.

Teens who "cyberbully" others via the Internet or cell phones are more likely to suffer from both physical and psychiatric troubles, and their victims are at heightened risk, too, a Finnish study finds.

The survey of almost 2,500 teens found that more than 7 percent of teens bullied other teens online, about 5 percent were targets of this aggressive behavior, and 5.4 percent said they were both bullies and bullied.

"People may wonder how similar teens in Finland are to teens in the U.S., but national research that I recently published indicates that rates of traditional bullying and victimization from bullying are very similar among kids in both countries," said Dr. Matthew Davis, an associate professor of pediatrics, internal medicine and public policy at the University of Michigan.

In fact, a recent U.S. survey of children aged 10 to 17 found that 12 percent were "aggressive" to someone else while online, 4 percent were victims of this type of online aggression, while 3 percent reported being both aggressors and targets.

The new study appears in the July [2010] issue of *Archives of General Psychiatry*.

As defined by the researchers, cyberbullying includes aggressive, intentional, repeated acts using mobile phones, computers (including e-mails and Facebook) or other electronic media against victims who cannot easily defend themselves.

Teens who were victims of cyberbullying were more likely to come from broken homes and have emotional, concentration and behavior problems.

A Spotlight on Cyberbullying

The widely publicized death in January [2010] of 15-year-old Phoebe Prince, a Massachusetts teen who took her life after months of relentless cyberbullying, swung a national spotlight on the issue. Parents have also become increasingly concerned about both bullying and their children's Internet safety, Davis said, and "for that reason, it is imperative that we track and address the problems of cyberbullying and cyberpredator behavior very actively in the near future."

In addition, the fact that about a third of teens in the United States and Finland report that they are victims of some type of bullying behavior "is a red flag that communities, schools, and families must respond more effectively to bullying, whether it occurs in person or electronically. This is an area that needs more real-world attention and action," Davis said.

For the study, a team led by Dr. Andre Sourander, from Turku University, collected data on 2,215 Finnish teens 13 to 16 years old. The teens were asked about cyberbullying and cybervictimization, as well as their overall health.

Teens who were victims of cyberbullying were more likely to come from broken homes and have emotional, concentration and behavior problems. These teens also found it harder to get along with others. In addition, they were prone to headaches, abdominal pain, sleeping problems and not feeling safe at school, the researchers found.

Cyberbullies were not without their own problems, however. Compared to teens who didn't engage in such behaviors, they were also more prone to suffering from emotional, concentration and behavior problems. In addition, they had trouble getting along with others and often suffered from hyperactivity and conduct problems. Cyberbullies also frequently smoked or got drunk, reported headaches, and were more prone to not feeling safe at school, the study found.

Teens who were both cyberbullies and cybervictims suffered from all of these conditions, Sourander's group found.

"Of those who had been victimized, one in four reported that it had resulted in fear for their safety," the researchers wrote. The feeling of being unsafe is probably worse in cyberbullying compared with traditional bullying, they added. That's because traditional bullying typically occurs on school grounds, so victims can at least feel safe within their homes.

With cyberbullying, however, victims are at risk 24 hours a day, seven days a week, the team noted.

Dealing with Cyberbullying

Richard Gallagher, director of the Parenting Institute at the NYU [New York University] Child Study Center in New York City, believes that schools, parents and children can all play a role in dealing with cyberbullying.

"Some schools are very concerned about this," he said. "And if they find out about it some schools are taking proactive action and there are consequences for the bully." But other schools aren't taking as active a role, Gallagher noted. "The proactive approach does seem to be helping with reducing the impact of bullying and teasing," he said. "So, I do think it is appropriate for schools to do this, but to be careful how they do it."

"In addition, most effective anti-bullying programs are ones that suggest that bystanders should be involved as well," Gallagher said. In these cases other children or parents who know someone is being bullied should report it to the school, he explained.

Another expert, Dr. Thomas Paul Tarshis, director of the Bay Area Children's Association in Cupertino, Calif., said the problem of cyberbullying is a growing one.

"The main place cyberbullying and cybervictimization begins from is the school," he said. "So it is in the school-peer relations where kids are likely to put pressure on someone, to taunt someone through instant messaging or Facebook."

Ideally, all schools should implement strict anti-bullying policies, but many are overwhelmed, he said. "Schools aren't even doing enough with standard bullying," he noted.

One positive of cyberbullying is that it leaves a data trial, Tarshis said. "So it's easier to get evidence of cyberbullying and it makes discipline and follow-through better."

7

Cyberbullying May Exacerbate Problems That Can Lead to Suicide

Sameer Hinduja and Justin W. Patchin

Sameer Hinduja, professor of criminology and criminal justice at Florida Atlantic University, is co-director with Justin W. Patchin of the Cyberbullying Research Center. Patchin is a criminal justice professor at University of Wisconsin-Eau Claire. Together they lecture and facilitate workshops on the causes and consequences of cyberbullying.

While cyberbullying alone is not likely to lead to youth suicide, it may worsen feelings of hopelessness in adolescents struggling with stress in their lives. Studies show that cyber and traditional bullying are both strong predictors of suicidal thoughts and behaviors among both victims and offenders. While few question that the nature and intensity of aggression has increased with the use of electronic communication technology, parents and school officials should take all forms of bullying seriously. Nevertheless, policymakers should also remember that the teens who committed suicide in high-profile cases had other emotional and social problems.

Youth suicide continues to be a significant public health concern in the United States. Even though suicide rates have decreased 28.5 percent among young people in recent

Sameer Hinduja and Justin W. Patchin, "Cyberbullying and Suicide," Cyberbulling Research Summary, 2010, pp. 206–221. www.springer.com. Copyright © 2010 by Cyberbullying Research Center. Reproduced by permission of the authors. Note: This is an abbreviated version of a full-length journal article entitled "Bullying, Cyberbullying, and Suicide," which was published in the journal *Archives of Suicide Research*, 14(3), 206–221.

years, upward trends were identified in the 10- to 19-year-old age group. In addition to those who successfully end their life, many other adolescents strongly think about and even attempt suicide.

The Bullying-Suicide Link

One factor that has been linked to suicidal ideation is experience with bullying. That is, youth who are bullied, or who bully others, are at an elevated risk for suicidal thoughts, attempts, and completed suicides. The reality of these links has been strengthened through research showing how experience with peer harassment (most often as a target but also as a perpetrator) contributes to depression, decreased self-worth, hopelessness, and loneliness—all of which are precursors to suicidal thoughts and behavior.

Without question, the nature of adolescent peer aggression has evolved due to the proliferation of information and communications technology. There have been several high-profile cases involving teenagers taking their own lives in part because of being harassed and mistreated over the Internet, a phenomenon we have termed *cyberbullicide*—suicide indirectly or directly influenced by experiences with online aggression. While these incidents are isolated and do not represent the norm, their gravity demands deeper inquiry and understanding. Much research has been conducted to determine the relationship between *traditional* bullying and suicidal ideation, and it can be said with confidence that a strong relationship exists. Based on what we found in the extant literature base, we sought to determine if suicidal ideation was also linked to experiences with *cyberbullying* among offenders and targets.

Looking at the Results

In our recent research involving approximately 2,000 randomly-selected middle-schoolers from one of the most populous school districts in the United States, 20% of respondents reported seriously thinking about attempting suicide (19.7% of females; 20.9% of males), while 19% reported attempting suicide (17.9% of females; 20.2% of males). This is comparable to other studies focusing on adolescent populations. With regard to traditional bullying, prevalence rates for individual behaviors ranged from 6.5% to 27.7% for offending and from 10.9% to 29.3% for victimization. The most common form of bullying offending reported by respondents was: "I called another student mean names, made fun of or teased him or her in a hurtful way" (27.7%), while the most frequently-cited form of bullying victimization was: "Other students told lies or spread false rumors about me and tried to make others dislike me" (29.3%). With regard to cyberbullying, prevalence rates for individual behaviors ranged from 9.1% to 23.1% for offending and from 5.7% to 18.3% for victimization. The most commonly-reported form of cyberbullying offending was: "Posted something online about another person to make others laugh" (23.1%) while the most frequent form of victimization was: "Received an upsetting email from someone you know" (18.3%).

[C]yberbullying victims were 1.9 times more likely and cyberbullying offenders were 1.5 times more likely to have attempted suicide than those who were not cyberbullying victims or offenders.

With respect to bullying, all forms were significantly associated with increases in suicidal ideation among sample respondents. That is, youth who experienced traditional bullying or cyberbullying, as either an offender or a victim, scored higher on our suicidal ideation scale than those who had not experienced those two forms of peer aggression. Moreover, it appears that bullying and cyberbullying *victimization* was a stronger predictor of suicidal thoughts and behaviors than was bullying and cyberbullying *offending*.

Finally, we wanted to see if bullying and cyberbullying experiences were related to an increased likelihood of an adolescent attempting suicide. Results showed that all forms of peer aggression increased the likelihood that the respondent attempted suicide. Traditional bullying victims were 1.7 times more likely and traditional bullying offenders were 2.1 times more likely to have attempted suicide than those who were not traditional victims or offenders. Similarly, cyberbullying victims were 1.9 times more likely and cyberbullying offenders were 1.5 times more likely to have attempted suicide than those who were not cyberbullying victims or offenders.

[I]t is unlikely that experience with cyberbullying by itself leads to youth suicide. Rather, it tends to exacerbate instability and hopelessness in the minds of adolescents already struggling with stressful life circumstances.

Drawing Conclusions

The small but significant variation found in suicidal thoughts and actions based on bullying and cyberbullying suggests that all forms of adolescent peer aggression must be taken seriously—both at school and at home. As such, psychologists, counselors, and parents must continually monitor the online and offline behaviors of youth to reinforce the good and regulate the bad. In addition, the findings suggest that a suicide prevention and intervention component is essential within comprehensive bullying response programs implemented in schools. Without question, the topic is sensitive and its presentation should be age-appropriate, as students in all grade levels must understand the serious consequences associated with peer aggression. While suicide is an extreme response, proper discussion of its stark reality can vividly portray the extent of harm that peer harassment can exact.

It should be acknowledged that many of the teenagers who committed suicide after experiencing bullying or cyberbullying had other emotional and social issues going on in their lives. For example, one cyberbullicide victim attended special education classes in elementary school and struggled socially and academically. Another suffered from low self-esteem and depression and was on medication when she took her life. As mentioned earlier, it is unlikely that experience with cyberbullying *by itself* leads to youth suicide. Rather, it tends to exacerbate instability and hopelessness in the minds of adolescents already struggling with stressful life circumstances. Future research should identify and specifically assess the contributive nature of these stress-inducing experiences.

8

Parents Must Be More Involved to Address Cyberbullying

Jim Kouri

Jim Kouri, fifth vice president of the National Association of Chiefs of Police, served on the National Drug Task Force and trained police and security officers throughout the country. He writes for many police and crime magazines and appears as a commentator for TV and radio news and talk shows.

Cyberbullying is a serious problem affecting America's youth. Thus, parents should become aware of what their children are doing online. While many parents believe that they know about their children's online activities, polls show that 52 percent of children do not tell their parents what they are doing online. Some children fear that if they talk to their parents about cyberbullying behavior, their parents will revoke electronic privileges. Therefore, parents should be careful how they approach concerns about their children's online activity. Parents should be prepared to listen and not dismiss bullying claims. In addition, parents should be sure to save offensive texts and e-mail and share offending messages with school officials.

Bullying among children encompasses a variety of harmful behaviors that are repeated over time, according to behavioral science experts. It involves a real or perceived imbalance of power, with the more powerful child or group attacking those who are less powerful. It can take three forms: physical, verbal, and psychological.

A New Avenue for an Old Problem

Bullying, a form of violence among children, is common on school playgrounds, in neighborhoods, and in homes throughout the United States and around the world. Often occurring out of the presence of adults or in front of adults who fail to intercede, bullying has long been considered an inevitable and, in some ways, uncontrollable part of growing up. The Internet has offered bullies an additional avenue to exploit.

School bullying has come under intense public and media scrutiny recently amid reports that it may have been a contributing factor in shootings at Columbine High School in Littleton, CO, in 1999 and Santana High School in Santee, CA, in early 2001 and in other acts of juvenile violence including suicide. Bullying can affect the social environment of a school, creating a climate of fear among students, inhibiting their ability to learn, and leading to other antisocial behavior.

Nevertheless, through research and evaluation, successful programs to recognize, prevent, and effectively intervene in bullying behavior have been developed and replicated in schools across the country. These schools send the message that bullying behavior is not tolerated and, as a result, have improved safety and created a more inclusive learning environment.

A Problem for School-Age Children

Cyberbullying and sexting have become major problems facing school-age children, their parents as well as school personnel, according to Bridget Roberts-Pittman, Indiana State University assistant professor of counseling.

"With the increase in technological devices, children are now using such to harass and harm other children," said

Roberts-Pittman. "Many children have personal cell phones making it very easy to use these devices in that way. Communication in cyberspace also seems more anonymous and seems to require less responsibility on the part of the child committing the behavior."

While bullying has long posed problems for children, it has now moved to cyberspace. Surveys show as many as 25 percent of children are reporting being cyberbullied. Cyberbullying can be defined as the use of technological devices to deliberately harass or harm another person such as through e-mail, text messaging, instant messaging, cell phones and Internet social networking sites.

Sexting refers to sending sexually explicit photographs typically via a cell phone. At least 20 percent of teens said they have sent a sexually explicit photo through a cell phone.

Parents also need to be aware of what their children are doing in cyberspace.

A Need for Parental Awareness

"Teens and their parents are not aware of the serious nature of such an act and the potentially life-long consequences," Roberts-Pittman said of sexting.

In responding to cyberbullying and sexting issues, Roberts-Pittman said parents need to be aware of major changes in a child's behavior.

"Behavior change is a part of adolescence. However, a significant change could mean the child is dealing with a serious issue such a cyberbullying," she said. "Parents should be aware of signs such as anxiety, depression, their child not wanting to attend school or making a drastic decision such as quitting a sports team."

Parents also need to be aware of what their children are doing in cyberspace. While 93 percent of parents said they knew what their children were doing online, 52 percent of children said they do not tell their parents what they do online, according to Roberts-Pittman.

"Parents have a right to check their child's phone and Internet use," she said and suggested using software packages such as Spectorsoft or I Am Big Brother. "Parents need to talk to their children about cyberbullying and sexting. Children today are so saturated with technology that they might not even recognize the behavior as a serious problem."

Teens caught sexting can be charged with possession of or distribution of child pornography and be required to register as a sex offender for many years, up to 20 in Indiana.

"The Legislature has not caught up with technology," she said. "The best message for children is 'Don't do it.'"

"The collaboration between parents and school officials is critical to address the cyberbullying and sexting."

Steps Parents Can Take

Roberts-Pittman said parents can take steps to help their children if they are involved in sexting or cyberbullying. The first is to listen.

"It is critical that children feel heard and understood," she said. "Keeping an open dialogue about issues such as peers is not easy, but very important for children to know that they can talk to their parents."

She said children often do not talk to their parents because they are afraid of their parents revoking their cell phone or computer privileges. They also don't believe their parents have the technical knowledge to understand. They also fear their parents will say "I told you so."

A second step for parents to help their children is to know they have options, especially in responding to cyberbullying.

"They can and should talk to the police about harassment," Roberts-Pittman said. "If the information is posted on a social networking site, they can contact the site to have the information removed."

The third step is to save all of the texts and emails sent to the child.

"It seems to be the parent's natural tendency to encourage their child to ignore the information and delete but that is the opposite of what we want children to do," she said. "Information can be tracked and traced."

Also, parents of the child being bullied may want to address the cyberbullying with the parents of the child committing the bullying.

"I only encourage parents to do this if they have the saved information to share with the other parents," she said.

As a fourth step, Roberts-Pittman said parents should share the information with school personnel.

"The collaboration between parents and school officials is critical to address the cyberbullying and sexting," she said.

9

Physicians Should Screen for Cyberbully Victimization

Christine S. Moyer

Christine S. Moyer covers health and science for American Medical News, *a publication of the American Medical Association.*

Mental health professionals have noticed a rise in the problem of cyberbullying among America's children and adolescents. They therefore urge primary care physicians to screen their patients for cyberbullying and recommend that physicians also educate young patients on the topic. Teens are particularly vulnerable to cyberbullying as they are in the process of developing their self-image. In fact, cyberbullying victims who are less stable may be more vulnerable to depression. Physicians should also screen for cyberbullies. Bullies bully for a reason, and they may suffer from depression or experience abuse at home. Physicians who encounter cyberbullying should assure victims that they are not at fault and contact police about any credible threats.

A few years ago, patients of child and adolescent psychiatrist Niranjan Karnik, MD, PhD, began talking to him about online harassment. Some of the youths were teased on social networking sites. Others received threatening text messages.

A Growing Problem

Since then, such complaints have been on the rise at the University of Chicago clinic where Dr. Karnik works. To address the growing problem, he continues to ask about traditional bullying but has added a new topic to office visits—cyberbullying, in which technology is used to repeatedly harass an individual. The incidents can occur through e-mails, text messages, Twitter and social networking sites.

"We do see more of this happening, [partly because] it's so simple to do," said Dr. Karnik, assistant professor of psychiatry at the University of Chicago. "It doesn't require you to stand in front of a person to bully them."

Mental health professionals are urging primary care physicians to address this mounting problem with their young patients by educating them on the topic and screening for possible victims and perpetrators. They say leaving the issue unchecked can result in anxiety, depression and, in some instances, suicide among those involved.

Suicide rates for cyberbullying victims and perpetrators were above those of students not involved in the activity, just as the rates for victims and perpetrators of traditional bullying also were elevated, according to a July 2010 *Archives of Suicide Research* study based on 1,963 sixth- through eighth-graders in one of the largest school districts in the U.S. Cyberbullying has gained more public attention recently due to several high-profile suicides in 2010 that followed such harassment.

Although research indicates that cyberbullying seems to occur most frequently among teenagers, anyone who spends time online can be harassed, according to child and adolescent psychiatrists.

[P]ediatricians and family physicians should ask all of their patients if they use the Internet and have a cell phone.

Screening Patients

To help identify youths who are affected by such incidents, pediatricians and family physicians should ask all of their patients if they use the Internet and have a cell phone, said Boston psychiatrist Tristan Gorrindo, MD. Patients who answer "yes" to either question are vulnerable to being a cyberbully victim or perpetrator, he said.

Despite the growing prevalence and publicity of cyberbullying, many physicians are not yet seeing patients with complaints of such harassment, said Gwenn Schurgin O'Keeffe, MD, an executive committee member of the American Academy of Pediatrics' Council on Communications and Media. She said the topic won't be brought up in a doctor's office until primary care physicians ask patients about it.

"I recognize that doctors have a lot on their plate. This is all new for everybody. But everyone has to have a heightened sense of awareness that children are being bullied [with technology], and it's happening more than people want to admit," said Dr. O'Keeffe, a Hudson, Mass., pediatrician.

As Technology Spreads, Cyberbullying Follows

About 43% of teenagers age 13 to 17 reported being cyberbullied during the previous year, according to 2006 data from a National Crime Prevention Council survey. The council is a Virginia-based nonprofit that addresses the cause of crime and violence and aims to reduce it.

That study is among the most recent and widely cited on the prevalence of cyberbullying. But mental health experts estimate that these numbers have increased with the growth of mobile access to the Internet and the involvement of youths in technology at younger ages. In fact, many psychiatrists said the cyberbully victims they see in their practices are getting younger.

In 2009, 58% of 12-year-olds owned a cell phone, up from 18% in 2004, according to a survey of 800 adolescents by the Pew Research Center's Internet and American Life Project. Overall, 75% of teens age 12 to 17 had a cell phone in 2009.

Experts say the rise of social media is making cyberbullying more common. In 2009, 73% of teenagers who spent time online used a social networking site. The figure was 55% in 2006.

But even as younger children become more active online, cyberbullying probably will remain most problematic for teenagers, said Dr. Gorrindo, a child and adolescent psychiatrist at Massachusetts General Hospital in Boston.

He noted that the developmental task of teenagers is to figure out who they are. This group already has an unstable image of themselves, which can be further weakened by moving to a new school or uncertainty about their sexuality, he said.

Dr. Gorrindo stressed that for many individuals, cyberbullying is largely a nuisance and will not lead to suicide or other serious mental health issues. A 2006 *Pediatrics* study of 1,500 Internet users found 38% of 10- to 17-year-olds who were the target of Internet harassment reported "emotional distress."

But for adolescents who have a less stable sense of their identity, including individuals with mental health issues and those who are perceived as outsiders by their peers, cyberbullying can drive them deeper into depression.

"In children with these [types of] vulnerabilities, cyberbullying is probably worse" than traditional, face-to-face harassment, he said.

Dr. Gorrindo noted that taunts on social networking sites can be viewed by hundreds of Internet friends, compared with traditional bullying, which often is witnessed by a small group of people. Cyberbullying is difficult for victims to escape because the attacks can occur in private moments over a computer and through cell phones.

Identifying Victims and Perpetrators

To identify potential victims and perpetrators of such harassment, Dr. Gorrindo suggests that physicians ask all their patients who use the Internet what they do online. He recommends that physicians specifically inquire about whether they use social networking sites and ever felt as if they were harassed. Additionally, he said doctors should ask patients if they bully other people. Dr. Gorrindo, in his experience, said children will be honest and forthcoming with their answers.

"Like almost any disease, the earlier we recognize [cyberbullying] and treat it, almost without exception, the better the outcome will be."

Adolescent medicine specialist Elizabeth Alderman, MD, said that children bully others for a reason, which could include depression or abuse by a parent. If a patient admits to cyberbullying, physicians should help the individual identify his or her actions as a problem and then involve the parent or guardian in the situation, said Dr. Alderman, a professor of clinical pediatrics at Montefiore Medical Center and Albert Einstein College of Medicine in New York.

When patients acknowledge that they have been victims, doctors first should assure the individuals that it's not their fault and then determine their level of danger for self-harm or acts inflicted by others, said Dr. O'Keeffe, of the AAP [American Academy of Pediatrics].

She said patients who need counseling should be referred to a mental health professional. Physicians should urge families to contact police if threats made against a patient seem credible, she added.

"Like almost any disease, the earlier we recognize [cyberbullying] and treat it, almost without exception, the better the outcome will be," said Henry J. Gault, MD, a child and adolescent psychiatrist in Deerfield, Ill.

"If you can intervene, you can protect a child from a great deal of harm," he said.

10

Federal Law Requires Schools to Protect Children from Cyberbullying

Wendy J. Murphy

Wendy J. Murphy, an adjunct professor at the New England School of Law in Boston, is a victims' rights advocate and television legal analyst.

When student speech amounts to targeted harassment based on race, religion, ethnicity, or gender, schools must act. If schools fail to do so, this failure should be redressed in federal court as a violation of the victim's civil rights. Although cyberbullying frequently occurs off-campus, the harmful impact is often experienced in school where it interferes with the victim's education. While school speech is protected, harassing speech is not. Indeed, federal courts have held that "there is no constitutional right to be a bully." Schools should therefore punish cyberbullies as long as students know that that harassing speech is a violation of civil rights. Schools should connect their disciplinary codes to civil rights laws.

After South Hadley high school student Phoebe Prince took her own life, Massachusetts lawmakers scrambled to explain why they haven't yet passed a meaningful antibullying law.

They should be ashamed of themselves, but their foot-dragging should not distract us from pointing the primary finger of blame at South Hadley school officials. They knew the vicious behavior that pushed Phoebe Prince to commit suicide involved relentless verbal assaults from students who called the girl a "slut," "Irish slut" and other derogatory names based on gender. It was obviously bullying, but it was also severe, pervasive and gender-specific verbal torture, which is sexual harassment, thus a violation of Title IX—the federal civil rights law that has forbidden gender discrimination in schools since its enactment in the early 1970s.

Some forms of bullying don't rise to the level of discrimination, and even the most hateful comments cannot be prohibited in the real world because speech is constitutionally protected.

[E]ven if the harmful conduct occurs in a cyber-venue such as Facebook, school officials must step in.

No Constitutional Right to Bully

But schools are special places where speech *can* be regulated in certain circumstances, as when it amounts to targeted harassment based on race, religion, ethnicity, gender, etc. Almost all bullying falls under one of these protected class categories and can be redressed in federal court because, as one federal appeals court recently ruled, "intimidation by name calling" is not protected speech on campus. Schools are "expected to prevent it", the court said, because "there is no constitutional right to be a bully".

When Title IX applies, federal law mandates that schools take "prompt and effective" steps to stop sexual harassment. Yet South Hadley school officials did nothing "effective" to protect Phoebe because they treated the situation as simple bullying—which does not require schools to intervene.

Phoebe and her family could have insisted that the school handle the situation as a Title IX issue, and they could have used Title IX to get a restraining order against the bullies—which school officials would have been obligated to enforce on campus. But the public doesn't understand the relationship between Title IX and gender-specific bullying. We've all been misled to believe the primary goal of Title IX is to ensure that girls and boys have the same number of basketballs.

Sports equity is important, but the more compelling purpose of Title IX is the prevention of gender discrimination, including sexual harassment, sexual violence and bullying "based on" gender.

Schools rarely acknowledge sexual harassment when they see it, and even when they do, they avoid getting involved when some of the conduct occurs off-campus. They tell parents they only have jurisdiction over harassment that occurs "on campus" or in connection with a school-sponsored activity.

Nonsense.

The best way to stop bullies of all kinds is to make sure every school disciplinary code connects the dots between bullying and laws against targeted harassment.

Connecting Cyberbully Harassment to the School Environment

Title IX applies so long as there is a "nexus" between the harassment and the school environment. Thus, even if the harmful conduct occurs in a cyber-venue such as Facebook, school officials must step in. The test is not where did the speech originate but rather, where did the harmful effects land? If one student's off-campus harassment interferes with another student's on-campus education, schools have the right and the DUTY to do something "effective" about it.

Doing something "effective" includes punishing the harassers/bullies. But the failure of schools to inform all students that bullying *can* be a violation of federal civil rights laws will make punishment in South Hadley difficult. Schools can't punish students for doing something wrong unless they were on notice that it was against the rules. This fact alone is a strong argument in favor of better education efforts around the relationship between laws like Title IX and bullying.

The best way to stop bullies of all kinds is to make sure every school disciplinary code connects the dots between bullying and laws against targeted harassment. Since schools have had decades to get this done, and have failed, a lawsuit against South Hadley on the theory that school officials caused the death of Phoebe Prince by violating her rights under Title IX will help them put the dots together real fast.

Suing a public school is unpopular, but the needless death of a young girl is reason enough to do it in this case. Financial pain will change school culture better and more quickly than hand-wringing, new antibullying laws, revised training programs and even a ton of bad press.

A high profile lawsuit explaining why Phoebe Prince did not have to die will expose the truth about what happened in South Hadley, which will incentivize all schools to adopt more effective policies against all forms of harassment and bullying. A lawsuit will also help to educate parents and children about their rights.[1] It won't bring Phoebe back, but it will mean she didn't die in vain.

---

1. Citing a Massachusetts state law against discrimination in educational settings, the parents of Phoebe Prince did file a complaint in July 2010 accusing the school and school officials of failing to protect Phoebe from discrimination that amounted to sexual harassment. They did not file a federal Title IX complaint.

11

Schools Have the Right to Punish Cyberbullies

Nancy Willard

Nancy Willard, director of the Center for Safe and Responsible Internet Use, conducts workshops on policies and practices related to Internet use in schools and has written numerous articles on this subject. She is also the author of the book, Cyberbullying and Cyberthreats: Responding to the Challenge of Online Social Aggression, Threats, and Distress.

Schools have the right to punish cyberbullies for off-campus online bullying if it interferes with education. Unfortunately, in J.C. v. Beverly Hills Unified School District, *the judge, who came to the opposite conclusion, failed to consider cases that clearly address this issue. In one case the Circuit Court held that school intervention is warranted when disruptive speech interferes with educational performance and in another case that the constitution does not protect the speech of bullies. The judge also ignored cyberbullying experts who state that the emotional harm cyberbullies cause substantially interferes with school performance. As long as a school's disciplinary policy clearly explains that school officials will punish off-campus online behavior that disrupts school, school officials have the duty to do so.*

The United States District Court for the Central District of California has issued a disturbing decision in a cyberbullying case, *J.C. v. Beverly Hills Unified School District.*

Nancy Willard, "There Is No Constitutional Right to Be a Cyberbully: Analysis of *J.C. v. Beverly Hills Unified School District,*" Center for Safe and Responsible Internet Use, December 16, 2009. www.csriu.org. Copyright © 2009 by Center for Safe and Responsible Use of the Internet. Reproduced by permission.

An Inaccurate Legal Interpretation

Although the news coverage of the decision has indicated that the case determined that school officials do not have the right to impose discipline for student off-campus cyberbullying, this is an inaccurate interpretation of the decision. In all of the cases that have involved off-campus online student speech, including this decision, the courts have uniformly held that school officials have the authority to respond to student speech, regardless of geographic origin, under the standard enunciated in *Tinker v. Des Moines Independent Community School District* (1969). Under Tinker, school officials can restrict or respond to student speech if that speech has caused, or foreseeably will cause a substantial disruption at school or interference with the rights of students to be secure.

What presents concern about this decision is that in applying the *Tinker* standard to a situation involving a student online attack against another student, the District Court ruled school officials can only impose discipline if the speech has or foreseeably could cause violence or other substantial disruption *of school activities.* Judge Wilson dismissed the concerns of emotional harm inflicted on the student who was denigrated and the impact of this verbal aggression on her right to receive an education and feel secure at school. Thus, the ruling calls into question all disciplinary responses to student verbal aggression, whether occurring on- or off-campus.

There is no constitutional right to be a bully.

Guidance Not Considered

Fortunately, there is contrary guidance in several other leading Circuit Court student free speech cases that addressed discipline in the context of student bullying that were unfortunately not considered by the court.

The primary function of a public school is to educate its students; conduct that substantially interferes with the mission (including speech that substantially interferes with a student's educational performance) is, almost by definition, disruptive to the school environment. *Saxe v. State College Area Sch. Dist.* (2001).

Intimidation of one student by another, including intimidation by name calling, is the kind of behavior school authorities are expected to prevent. There is no constitutional right to be a bully. *Sypniewski v. Warren Hills Regional Board of Education* (2002).

The Court also determined that the school's disciplinary policy was unconstitutionally vague because they did [not] provide the student with fair notice that off-campus conduct could be regulated and disciplined. This decision should provide significant incentive for districts to review their policies to ensure that students are on notice that off-campus acts that substantial disrupt the school can be subject to a disciplinary consequence.

[S]chool officials must have the authority to respond to [cyberbullying] incidents and, if justified, remove offending students from school. . . .

The Facts of the Case

The facts in this case bear similarity to cyberbullying incidents that school officials are struggling to address with an unfortunate frequency. Plaintiff J.C. and several other students gathered at a local restaurant. Plaintiff recorded a short video of her friends talking about a classmate, C.C. One of Plaintiff's friends called C.C. a "slut," said that C.C. is "spoiled," talked about "boners," and used other profanity. During the video, J.C. is heard encouraging this student to continue to talk about C.C. In the evening on the same day, Plaintiff posted the video on the website "YouTube" from her home computer. She also contacted 5 to 10 students from the school and told them to look at the video. She also contacted C.C. and informed her of the video.

C.C. came to the middle school with her mother and spoke with school counselor. She was crying and told the counselor that she did not want to go to class. The counselor spent some time counseling C.C. and convincing her to go to class. J.C. and the other students involved in the incident were called to the office. J.C. was suspended for 2 days. The father of the student who spoke on the video came to school and viewed the video and removed her from school for that day. It was estimated that approximately half of the 8th grade students had seen the video.

Research addressing cyberbullying has consistently revealed that these incidents can be exceptionally emotionally traumatic and frequently are related or contribute to school failure, school avoidance, violence at school—and sometimes youth suicide. To protect the well-being of youth, school officials must have the authority to respond to these incidents and, if justified, remove offending students from school for a period of time. . . .

Dismissing the Impact of Emotional Harm

The Court dismissed the emotional harm suffered by C.C. Most notably and highly illogically, the Court downplayed the significance of harm caused by this cruel video by stating that "while C.C. was undoubtedly upset, it took the school counselor, at most, 20–25 minutes to calm C.C. down and convince her to go to class."

The Court failed to note the context of C.C.'s decision. Her willingness to go to class was predicated on the fact that she knew that the school officials were intending to call the aggressors to the office and deal with the situation. The fact that the school officials at Beverly Vista School responded promptly and effectively to this situation was held against the district. Due to the district's effective disciplinary actions, the foreseeable significant interference with C.C.'s ability to participate in school activities was prevented!

Let's replay this situation with Judge Wilson's resolution. C.C. comes to the counselor reporting that she is being targeted by students who are calling her a "slut" and spreading nasty rumors about her. The counselor's response is that she is being emotionally fragile and since no violence has yet occurred nor is predicted there is nothing the school can or will do and she should go back to class. At its essential core, this is what the ruling of Judge Wilson deems to be an appropriate school response.

A Lack of Insight into the Problem of Bullying

Judge Wilson further displayed his abject lack of insight into the problems of bullying and the serious consequences of bullying on the emotional well-being and educational success of students. Examples include:

> The Court does not take issue with Defendants' argument that young students often say hurtful things to each other, and that students with limited maturity may have emotional conflicts over even minor comments. However, to allow the School to cast this wide a net and suspend a student simply because another student takes offense to their speech, without any evidence that such speech caused a substantial disruption of the school's activities, runs afoul of *Tinker*.

> ...(T)he School's decision must be anchored in something greater than one individual student's difficult day (or hour) on campus.

> ...(N)o one could seriously challenge that thirteen-year-olds often say mean-spirited things about one another, or that a teenager likely will weather a verbal attack less ably

75

than an adult. The Court accepts that C.C. was upset, even hysterical, about the YouTube video, and that the School's only goal was to console C.C. and to resolve the situation as quickly as possible.

The Court cannot uphold school discipline of student speech simply because young persons are unpredictable or immature, or because, in general, teenagers are emotionally fragile and may often fight over hurtful comments.

Judge Wilson's comments and interpretation of this situation flies in the face of all bullying prevention guidance, thus reinforcing the wisdom of the guidance provided in *Tinker* that the "Court has repeatedly emphasized the need for affirming the comprehensive authority of the States and of school officials, consistent with fundamental constitutional safeguards, to prescribe and control conduct in the schools."

Why Did the Decision Go Off Track?

One reason this decision went off-track is likely the limited legal guidance related to the constitutionality of a school response when a student is bullying, or being verbally aggressive, towards another student. One reason for the lack of case law is likely that there are very few attorneys such J.C.'s father, Evan Cohen, who filed the case, who are inclined to file a law suit against a school district arguing that students should have a First Amendment right to torment and harass other students.

The other reason is that the arguments in this case appeared to be framed in the context of the recent online, off-campus student speech cases—with the failure to note the critical difference between these other cases and the situation in Beverly Hills School. All of the other off-campus online cases involved student online speech that targeted school staff. Thus, the issue of whether such speech had caused a substantial disruption of school activities was relevant in those cases. There have not been any other cases involving speech targeting other students.

What Should School Officials Do?

At first glance, this ruling may appear to suggest to school officials that they should refrain from intervening in any bullying or cyberbullying situations, on or off-campus, absent evidence of the potential for violence or a substantial disruption *of school activities.* This interpretation would essentially require a rewriting of most school district bullying prevention policies, many of which are dictated by state statute. Because the Court framed its decision in the context the ability of school officials to respond to speech regardless of geographic origin, but determined that the substantial disruption must be of school activities and if the Court's conclusion is correct, then this calls into question the constitutionality of all school bullying prevention statutes and policies.

Alternatively, districts could, under guidance from their legal council, continue to rely on the guidance set forth in *Saxe* and *Sypniewski* and respond to situations where the severe or pervasive behavior of one student has or could significantly interfere with the security of another student—regardless of the geographic origin of such speech.

The arena where some attorneys appear to be inclined to pursue legal action are those situations involving off-campus, online speech—cyberbullying. When a school official intends to impose a formal disciplinary response on a student for off-campus harmful speech that has targeted another student, the focus—and evidence retention—must be on the potential for that speech to significantly interfere with the targeted student's educational performance and emotional security at school. It is likely that school officials should be prepared to address this question based both on the subjective perspective of the target, as well as an objective analysis. This is also in accord with

77

guidance from *Saxe* and *Sypniewski*. These are the kinds of situations where evidence retention related to the targeted student's subjective response, as well as retention of all harmful material, will be critical.

12

College Campus Cyberbullying Laws Threaten Free Speech

Foundation for Individual Rights in Education

The mission of the Foundation for Individual Rights in Education (FIRE) is to defend individual rights at America's colleges and universities and educate the public and American communities about the threats to these rights on America's campuses. FIRE defends freedom of speech, legal equality, due process, religious liberty, and sanctity of conscience.

Anti-bullying bills drafted in response to high-profile cyberbullying tragedies threaten free speech on college campuses. These bills redefine harassment in contravention of Supreme Court standards that require behavior to be offensive to a reasonable person. As a result, those who wish to silence speech that they oppose can determine what campus speech will be banned, even if a reasonable person would not find the speech offensive. In the past, college administrators have been unable to fairly and rationally enforce unclear speech policies. Thus, vague standards in anti-bullying bills effectively censor unpopular ideas and suppresses open debate. Such draconian laws are unnecessary since policies to protect students from discriminatory harassment are already in place.

An "anti-bullying" bill introduced in Congress last week [November, 2010] gravely threatens free speech on America's college campuses. Despite the bill's admirable intention of preventing future tragedies, the Foundation for Individual Rights in Education (FIRE) has determined that the bill is at odds with the Supreme Court's carefully crafted definition of harassment and would require colleges to violate the First Amendment.

Policing Student Speech

"Tyler Clementi was subjected to an unconscionable violation of privacy, but that conduct was already criminal and prohibited by every college in America," FIRE President Greg Lukianoff said. "For decades, colleges have used vague, broad harassment codes to silence even the most innocuous speech on campus. The proposed law requires universities to police even more student speech under a hopelessly vague standard that will be a disaster for open debate and discourse on campus. And all this in response to student behavior that was already illegal."

After Senator Frank Lautenberg and Representative Rush Holt introduced the "Tyler Clementi Higher Education Anti-Harassment Act," Senator Lautenberg declared that "it is time for our colleges to put policies on the books that would protect students from harassment." But such policies are already in place. For decades, colleges that receive federal funding have been required to maintain policies that address discriminatory harassment under Titles VI and IX of the Civil Rights Act of 1964.

The bill, which would amend the Higher Education Act, flies in the face of that very law. When Congress reauthorized the Act in 2008, it added a "sense of Congress" provision noting that "an institution of higher education should facilitate the free and open exchange of ideas."

Flouting Supreme Court Definitions

In contrast, the bill redefines harassment in a manner that is at odds with the Supreme Court's exacting definition of student-on-student harassment, which successfully balances the need to respond to extreme behavior with the importance of free speech on campus. In *Davis v. Monroe County Board of Education* (1999), the Court defined student-on-student harassment as conduct that is "so severe, pervasive, and objectively offensive, and that so undermines and detracts from the victims' educational experience, that the victim-students are effectively denied equal access to an institution's resources and opportunities." This definition has been relied upon by courts for more than a decade and has been adopted by many institutions across the country, including the entire University of California system.

Those concerned about speech rights on the Internet have great reason to worry. . . .

Flouting the Supreme Court's carefully crafted balance, the bill removes the requirement that the behavior in question be objectively offensive. The loss of this crucial "reasonable person" standard means that those most interested in silencing viewpoints they don't like will effectively determine what speech should be banned from campus. Unconstitutional definitions of "harassment" have already provided the most commonly abused rationale justifying censorship, having been applied to a student magazine at Tufts University that published true if unflattering facts about Islam, a Brandeis professor who used an epithet in order to explain its origins and condemn its use as a slur, and even a student at an Indiana college simply for publicly reading a book.

Because this bill has the potential to be a powerful tool for censorship, it would likely be ruled unconstitutional were it to become law. Indeed, since 1989 there have been at least sixteen successful challenges to campus codes that included similarly broad and vague harassment provisions. Every one of those lawsuits has resulted in the challenged policy either being declared unconstitutional or revised as part of an out-of-court settlement. If passed, the bill is likely to violate students' rights while leading colleges into expensive, embarrassing, and unsuccessful litigation.

"What happened to Tyler Clementi was already illegal. This bill cannot prevent future students from breaking the law, but it surely will provide students and administrators with new tools to punish views or expression they simply dislike. FIRE's experience demonstrates that when speech is not unambiguously protected, censorship and punishment of unpopular views follows," Lukianoff said.

Enforcing Unclear Policies

The bill also fails to define what constitutes a "hostile or abusive" educational environment, leaving that determination to college administrators. Unfortunately, FIRE's extensive experience defending student speech demonstrates that college administrators are often incapable of enforcing unclear policies governing student speech either fairly or rationally. FIRE's case archive provides hundreds of examples of students and faculty members who have faced censorship, investigation, or punishment for parody, satire, speaking out against campus policies or public figures, and discussing important issues facing our society through protest and even through art.

Those concerned about speech rights on the Internet also have great reason to worry, as the bill requires university harassment policies to cover behavior that occurs online or off campus—anywhere in the world. In practice, this requirement is likely to compel universities to monitor student behavior in unprecedented ways—including close and comprehensive monitoring of social networking sites like Facebook and Twitter—in order to ward off potential lawsuits.

"For over a decade, FIRE has been successfully fighting the illiberal influence of speech codes at our nation's colleges and universities. But this bill threatens the significant progress made by FIRE and those students, faculty, alumni, and citizens that share our commitment to free speech on campus," said Will Creeley, FIRE's Director of Legal and Public Advocacy. "We must not let tragedy serve as a justification for rolling back the First Amendment [the bill never became law]."

13

Definitions in Laws to Prevent Cyberbullying Are Too Broad

John Cox

John Cox is senior editor of Network World, *a news magazine for information technology professionals.*

Broad definitions in online anti-bullying bills drafted in response to high-profile cyberbullying tragedies would turn offensive political speech into a crime. Failure to effectively define "severe emotional distress" and "hostile behavior" could lead to anomalous results. For example, speech by a blogger who questions a politician's integrity might be emotionally distressing. However, while hostile, such speech is necessary to public debate. Nevertheless, anti-bullying bills might turn the blogger into a criminal. Experts argue that parents and school officials are in the best position to handle most cyberbullying cases. In a democratic society in which speech is protected by the First Amendment, sweeping legislation that fails to clearly define criminal behavior is unwarranted.

A little-noticed bill re-introduced in Congress last month [April 2009] would make the use of popular electronic communications a felony if "the intent is to coerce, intimidate, harass, or cause substantial emotional distress to a person."

Turning Flamers into Felons

Given the free-wheeling exchanges that characterize everything from SMS [short message service] text messages and instant messaging, to blogs and Web site comments, the broadly written bill potentially could turn a lot of flamers and bloggers into felons. If convicted, they would face fines (no amounts given) and prison sentences up to two years.

The bill is H.R. 1966, filed April 2 by Rep. Linda Sanchez, a liberal Democrat for California's 39th district, a horseshoe-shaped patch around Los Angeles, from Whittier through Ceritos to Lynnwood. She was joined by 14 other congressmen. It's been referred to the House Committee on the Judiciary.

Criticism from the Online Community

The bill has recently begun to receive attention, much of it critical, in the online community. Greg Pollowitz, at National Review Online's Media Blog, labeled it the "Censorship Act of 2009."

In fact, some of the comments could even be construed as intended to cause emotional distress under the bill's loosely defined language. Sanchez earlier this week [May 3–9, 2009] sought to explain and defend the proposal online at HuffingtonPost.com, a political blog that is generally considered liberal. One response to her post was by "radmul," who wrote, "No offense congresswoman but you can't handle prosecuting war criminals for torture so you have no right to bring your lack of ethics to the Web." Another comment, from "dubster," attacked still another poster who blamed the Megan Meier tragedy on "bad parenting": "I detest jerks like you, that can't comprehend the gravity and severity of certain things."

HR 1966 is Sanchez' second attempt (she first filed in May 2008) to enact the "Megan Meier Cyberbullying Prevention Act," a reference to a Missouri 13-year-old who in 2007 killed herself, apparently in despair over a bullying campaign organized against her on MySpace. A federal grand jury brought indictments against one of the teens involved, but the trial jury reduced three of the four felony counts to misdeameanors, and deadlocked on the fourth.[1]

Incidents like these have spawned local school policies and state laws against cyberbullying. At least 13 states have passed laws, including California earlier this year [2009].[2] But many of these require only administrative actions, such as suspending or expelling students. And all of them raise the issue of where to draw the line between protecting kids from electronic harassment and protecting the right to free speech.

> *"The [cyberbullying] law, if enacted, would clearly be facially overbroad (and probably unconstitutionally vague), and would thus be struck down. . . ."*

A Broad Definition

Given the potential First Amendment issues, the language in HR 1966 is as brief as it is broad. It reads:

(a) Whoever transmits in interstate or foreign commerce any communication, with the intent to coerce, intimidate, harass, or cause substantial emotional distress to a person, using electronic means to support severe, repeated, and hostile behavior, shall be fined under this title or imprisoned not more than two years, or both.

The bill defines "communication" as "the electronic transmission, between or among points specified by the user, of in-

1. Lori Drew, the woman indicted, was not a teen but the adult mother of a friend of Megan Meier. Drew, along with an employee and her daughter created a fake MySpace profile as a 16-year-old boy they named Josh Evans. The goal was to get retribution for alleged gossip about Drew's daughter. Meier and "Josh" became close online friends, but the messages changed and "Josh" accused Meier of being a bad person. Shortly before her suicide, one message said, "The world would be a better place without you." Although Drew was indicted and convicted in federal court, the case against her was overturned.
2. As of January 26, 2011, all fifty states have passed laws addressing cyberstalking, cyberharassment and/or cyberbullying. Some specifically redress these activities while others include electronic communication in already established harassment laws.

formation of the user's choosing, without change in the form or content of the information as sent and received."

"Electronic means" is defined as "any equipment dependent on electrical power to access an information service, including email, instant messaging, blogs, Web sites, telephones, and text messages."

HR 1966, formally an amendment to Title 18, "Crimes and Criminal Procedure," of the U.S. Code, does not define any other term, including "severe emotional distress," "hostile" or even "behavior."

Questioning the Law's Constitutionality

"The law, if enacted, would clearly be facially overbroad (and probably unconstitutionally vague), and would thus be struck down on its face under the First Amendment," wrote Eugene Volokh, the Gary T. Schwartz Professor of Law at UCLA School of Law, and blogger in chief at The Volokh Conspiracy, an online legal blog.

Volokh offered six quick sketches of the kinds of activities that could be prosecuted if HR 1966 becomes law, including trying to pressure' a politician, organizing a boycott against a company with whose policies you disagree, or even sending angry e-mails to an unfaithful lover.

A blogger trying to coerce an elected official into voting one way on a bill repeatedly posts "using a hostile tone" about what a "hypocrite/campaign promise breaker/fool" the official would be if he voted the other way, Volokh writes. "I am transmitting in interstate commerce a communication with the intent to coerce using electronic means (a blog) 'to support severe, repeated, and hostile behavior'—unless, of course, my statements aren't seen as 'severe,' a term that is entirely undefined and unclear. Result: I am a felon, unless somehow my 'behavior' isn't 'severe,'" Vokokh writes.

A woman discovers her lover is unfaithful and wants him to "feel like the scumbag he is," Volokh writes. If she sends her unfaithful lover two hostile e-mail messages telling him that in no uncertain terms, even without threatening violence, she "is transmitting communications with the intent to cause substantial emotional distress, using electronic means 'to support severe, repeated, and hostile behavior,'" Volokh writes.

[T]he [cyberbullying] bill's vagueness works against what it's trying to accomplish.

Garnering Little Support

To say the Sanchez bill has not yet garnered widespread support, or even attention, is an understatement. For example, even the Megan Meier Foundation appears unaware of the bill bearing the teenager's name: There is no reference to HR 1966 on the Web site. The Foundation's mission is to "bring awareness, education, and promote change to children, parents and educators in response to the ongoing bullying and cyberbullying in our children's daily environment."

Cyberbullying.us, a blog by two criminal justice professors to focus on "identifying the causes and consequences of online harassment," this week [May, 2009] also took note of the bill's flaws. "As I have stated before, I am not convinced that a state or federal law which criminalizes cyberbullying is necessarily the best approach," writes Justin Patchin, assistant professor of criminal justice, Department of Political Science at the University of Wisconsin-Eau Claire. "The vast majority of all cyberbullying can be effectively handled informally—by parents, educators, and other community members. In the rare event that a cyberbullying incident rises to a level warranting criminal intervention, we already have existing laws which can be utilized (stalking, criminal harassment, felonious assault, etc.)."

In an e-mail, Patchin's co-blogger, Sameer Hinduja, assistant professor with the Department of Criminology and

Criminal Justice, Florida Atlantic University, says the bill's vagueness works against what it's trying to accomplish.

"We need to render more concrete many of the clauses in the bill—we can't just assume that a reasonable person will feel the same way about every cyberbullying case that surfaces," Hinduja says. "Volokh's examples in his recent blog underscore the variety of scenarios subject to differing interpretations. Plus—just like with the sexual predator craze—societal and governmental sentiment towards the phenomenon will vary based on sensationalistic news stories and emotion. That will lead to inconsistent justice."

In her *Huffington Post* commentary this week [May 3-9, 2009], Sanchez begins by appealing to a sense of justice and to the defense of children.

"If you were walking down the street and saw someone harassing a child, would you just walk by and look the other way? If that person was telling the child the world would be better off if they just killed themselves, would you ignore it?" she writes. "This is what is happening on the Internet except it is more painful, and can be more abusive because of the faceless anonymity the web provides. Bullies are using technology in ways we could not have imagined only years ago, and studies show that outdated and erroneous beliefs that bullying is 'harmless' downplay its true seriousness."

Volokh critiqued Sanchez' defense in an e-mail response to a *Network World* inquiry . . . , again focusing on the First Amendment implications. Using "vulnerable children" to justify the law, as Sanchez does, obscures the fact that "nothing in the law [HR 1966] is at all limited to children," he says.

"Nor is it limited to individually targeted statements; it also covers newspaper articles on the Web, blog posts, and a wide range of other speech aimed at the public," Volokh says. "Sanchez also twice mentions the 'anonymity' of the Internet, but the [proposed] law is not at all limited to anonymous statements."

There are constitutionally recognized limits on free speech, Sanchez argues in *Huffington Post.* "Current Supreme Court jurisprudence already recognizes some reasonable regulation of speech is consistent with the First Amendment," she writes. "For example, the Court has found that true threats, commercial speech, slander, and libel can be reasonably restricted consistent with the Constitution."

Constitutionally Protected Speech

"[I]t's true that the Court has recognized that true threats of violence are legally punishable," responds Volokh. "But that narrow exception hardly applies to 'severe, repeated, and hostile' speech that's 'inten[ded] to coerce, . . . harass, or cause substantial emotional distress.' In fact, the Court has repeatedly held that even speech that's coercive—for instance, through fear of social ostracism—and extremely distressing is constitutionally protected, even against mere civil liability. See *NAACP v. Claiborne Hardware* (1982); *Hustler Magazine v. Falwell* (1988). The Court has never accepted the notion that the narrow and historically recognized exceptions to protection [of speech] justify a broad range of 'reasonable regulation of speech.'"

Sanchez notes that "Slander and libel law provide for different standards when the injured party is a public official or private person, and nothing in the Megan Meier Cyberbullying Prevention Act attempts to override that principle."

"But nothing in her proposal would draw any distinctions between public and private figures," Volokh says. "Nor would that be adequate, because even emotionally distressing speech about private figures is often constitutionally protected, as *Claiborne* and many other cases make clear."

The Problem with Judicial Discretion

HR 1966 emphasizes granting "discretion" for judges and juries "to recognize the difference between an annoying chain email, a righteously angry political blog post, or a miffed text to an ex-boyfriend and serious, repeated, hostile communications made with the intent to harm," Sanchez writes.

But such broad discretion is problematic, and for good reason, according to Volokh. ". . . [T]o the extent that Sanchez relies on case-by-case judicial and jury discretion, First Amendment law makes absolutely clear that one can't just rely on that," he says. "If the law [i.e., HR 1966] is said to be constitutional because it's narrowly limited, the limiting principles must be present in the law itself, rather than just being left to judges and juries to impose based on their own sense of what should be protected."

"More importantly, Sanchez draws a false dichotomy between 'a righteously angry political blog post' or 'a miffed text to an ex-boyfriend' [on the one hand] and 'serious, repeated, hostile communications made with the intent to harm' [on the other]," Volokh says. "What about serious, repeated, hostile righteously angry political blog posts made with the intent to coerce a politician to change her policies, or to substantially distress a politician whom the speaker is angry at, and the felonious 'serious, repeated, hostile communications made with the intent to harm'? What about serious, repeated, hostile messages to an ex-boyfriend explaining how much he has hurt you?"

In her online post, Sanchez writes that she "consulted with a variety of experts and law professors in crafting this bill to preserve our American freedom of speech and protect victims of cyberbullying."

"I would like to see even one statement from her 'variety of experts and law professors' that would explain how this law is constitutional," Volokh says [the bill never became law].

14

Requiring Internet Companies to Police Cyberbullying Is Unrealistic

Dan Whitcomb

Dan Whitcomb is a correspondent for Reuter's, a global news agency.

Although people value Internet freedom, high-profile cyberbullying tragedies have led some to hold Internet companies such as Google and Facebook, accountable for content on their websites. Holding Internet companies accountable, however, would require these companies to review everything posted on their sites, which is impossible. The alternative, restricting the content posted on their sites, would sacrifice Internet freedom. The online community claims that sites such as Facebook are self-regulating—the social networking site removes offensive content reported by users. Nevertheless, in a society where expectations of corporate social responsibility are high, Internet companies may be expected to do the impossible.

The Internet was built on freedom of expression. Society wants someone held accountable when that freedom is abused. And major Internet companies like Google and Facebook are finding themselves caught between those ideals.

Although Google, Facebook and their rivals have enjoyed a relatively "safe harbor" from prosecution over user-generated content in the United States and Europe, they face a public that increasingly is more inclined to blame them for cyberbullying and other online transgressions.

A Surprising Verdict

Such may have been the case when three Google executives were convicted in Milan, Italy on February 24 [2010] over a bullying video posted on the site—a verdict greeted with horror by online activists, who fear it could open the gates to such prosecutions and ultimately destroy the Internet itself.

Journalist Jeff Jarvis suggested on his influential BuzzMachine blog that the Italian court, which found Google executives guilty of violating the privacy of an autistic boy who was taunted in the video, was essentially requiring websites to review everything posted on them.

"The practical implication of that, of course, is that no one will let anyone put anything online because the risk is too great," Jarvis wrote. "I wouldn't let you post anything here. My ISP (Internet Service Provider) wouldn't let me post anything on its services. And that kills the Internet."

A seemingly stunned Chris Thompson, writing for *Slate,* said simply: "The mind reels at this medieval verdict."

Google and Facebook . . . seek to reconcile demands for accountability with the impossibility of monitoring everything posted on their sites.

Policemen of the Internet

And Matt Sucherman, a Google vice president and general counsel, wrote in a blog post that the company was "deeply troubled" by the case, saying it "attacks the very principles of freedom on which the Internet is built."

Legal experts have been more sanguine, saying the verdict in Milan will most likely end up an outlier—unable to stand the scrutiny even of the Italian appeals courts, never mind setting legal precedents elsewhere.

But in sentencing the executives to six-month suspended jail terms, the court may have seized on a growing desire to hold Internet companies responsible for the content posted by users.

"I actually think that this is probably not a watershed moment because the Google convictions violate European law and ultimately they will be overturned," said John Morris, general counsel for the Washington, D.C.-based Center for Democracy and Technology.

"Having said that, yes we are quite worried about the trend in other countries to suggest Internet service providers and Web sites should be the policemen of the Internet," Morris said.

If the trend takes hold, it could put the companies on the defensive, forcing them to spend more time defending such cases or fending off calls to restrict content in some way.

China polices the web and demands cooperation from web companies, while the United States has stuck up for Internet freedom in the face of censorship by more repressive governments.

But social pressure often comes from the ground up, as Facebook recently found out in Australia.

In that case Facebook pages set up in tribute to two children murdered in February, 8-year-old Trinity Bates and 12-year-old Elliott Fletcher, were quickly covered with obscenities and pornography, prompting calls for the social network to be more accountable for its content.

"To have these things happen to Facebook pages set up for the sole purpose of helping these communities pay tribute to young lives lost in the most horrible ways adds to the grief already being experienced," Queensland Premier Ann Bligh wrote to Facebook founder and CEO Mark Zuckerberg in a letter released to the Australian media.

"I seek your advice about whether Facebook can do anything to prevent a recurrence of these types of sickening incidents," Bligh said in the letter.

A Facebook spokeswoman responded that the popular social network, which has more than 400 million users worldwide, had rules to check content and that any reports of hate or threats would be quickly removed.

"Facebook is highly self-regulating and users can and do report content that they find questionable or offensive," the spokeswoman, Debbie Frost, said.

The MySpace Suicide

Calls for prosecution of cyber-bullying first reached a peak with the case of a suburban mother accused of driving a lovelorn 13-year-old girl, Megan Meier, to suicide in 2006 by tormenting her with a fake MySpace persona.

Lori Drew, the mother of a girl with whom Meir had quarreled, was found guilty of misdemeanor federal charges in a case dubbed the "MySpace Suicide" in the U.S. media, but a judge later dismissed her conviction on the grounds that the prosecution was selective the law unconstitutionally vague.

But Meier's death and a series of child exploitation cases linked to News Corp's MySpace brought pressure on the site to increase its security measures and may have cost it in its apparently losing rivalry with Facebook for social network dominance.

Such issues point to the business risks for the likes of Google and Facebook as they seek to reconcile demands for accountability with the impossibility of monitoring everything posted on their sites.

"We are a society that expects companies and people of authority to take responsibility, not only for their own actions but for the actions of those beneath them," said Karen North, director of the Annenberg Program on Online Communities at the University of Southern California.

"The difficulty is, we've created an Internet culture where people are invited to put up content, but the responsibility falls in both directions," North said. "(On the Internet) we all share the responsibility to monitor the content that we find and for our societal standards to be maintained."

Organizations to Contact

The editors have compiled the following list of organizations concerned with the issues debated in this book. The descriptions are derived from materials provided by the organizations. All have publications or information available for interested readers. The list was compiled on the date of publication of the present volume; names, addresses, phone and fax numbers, and e-mail and Internet addresses may change. Be aware that many organizations take several weeks or longer to respond to inquiries, so allow as much time as possible.

American Civil Liberties Union (ACLU)
125 Broad St., 18th Floor, New York, NY   10004
website: www.aclu.org

The ACLU works to uphold civil rights, focusing specifically on issues related to free speech, equal protection, due process, and privacy. The ACLU takes on court cases and related rulings that address the definition of these civil liberties; in recent years ACLU court cases have addressed issues such as student cell phone privacy at school and discipline of students for off-campus cyberbullying. On its website the ACLU publishes blogs, testimony, articles, and reports on protecting Internet speech while combating cyberbullying, including "Free Speech and 'Cyber-bullying'" and "ACLU Statement Submitted to a Subcommittee hearing on Cyberbullying."

Berkman Center for Internet and Society
23 Everett Street, 2nd Floor, Cambridge, MA   02138
(617) 495-7547 • fax: (617) 495-7641
e-mail: cyber@law.harvard.edu
website: http://cyber.law.harvard.edu

The center conducts research on legal, technical, and social developments in cyberspace and assesses the need or lack thereof for laws and sanctions. It publishes a monthly newsletter, *The Filter*, blog posts, and articles based on the center's research efforts, many of which are available on its website, including the final report of the Internet Safety Technical Task Force, *Enhancing Child Safety & Online Technologies* and "Insights on Cyberbullying: An Interview with a Digital Native," a news report from Berkman's Digital Natives Reporters in the Field.

Cato Institute
1000 Massachusetts Ave. NW, Washington, DC   20001-5403
(202) 842-0200 • fax: (202) 842-3490
e-mail: cato@cato.org
website: www.cato.org

The Cato Institute is a libertarian public policy research foundation that aims to limit the role of government and to protect civil liberties. The institute publishes the quarterlies, *CATO Journal* and *Regulation*, and the bimonthly *Cato Policy Report*. Its website publishes selections from these and other publications, including congressional testimony "Concerning The Megan Meier Cyberbullying Prevention Act (H.R. 1966); The Adolescent Web Awareness Requires Education Act (H.R. 3630)" and a video in which CATO's Harvey Silverglate discussions cyberbullying laws.

Center for Democracy and Technology (CDT)
1634 Eye St. NW, #1100, Washington, DC   20006
(202) 637-9800 • fax: 202.637.0968
website: www.cdt.org

CDT works to ensure that regulations concerning all current and emerging forms of technology are in accordance with democratic values, especially free expression and privacy. The center works to promote its ideals through research and education as well as grassroots movements. On its website CDT publishes articles papers, reports, and testimony, including "MySpace: Coming of Age for Coming of Age" and "Congressional Child Safety Bills Present Serious Constitutional Risks, and Some Opportunities for Effective Action."

Center for Safe and Responsible Internet Use (CSRIU)

474 W. Twenty-ninth Ave., Eugene, OR   97405
(541) 344-9125 • fax: 541-344-1481
e-mail: info@csriu.org
website: http://cyberbully.org

CSRIU is dedicated to educating parents, educators, and policymakers about the most effective methods of encouraging safe and responsible Internet use by children and teens. The center emphasizes the importance of equipping youth with the knowledge and personal strength to make good decisions that will help them avoid potentially harmful situations when using the Internet. Copies of reports by CSRIU executive director Nancy Willard, such as "Cyberbullying Legislation and Policies," "I Can't See You—You Can't See Me," "A Briefing for Educators: Online Social Networking Communities and Youth Risk," and "Student's Guide to Cyberbullying" are available on its website.

Electronic Frontier Foundation (EFF)

454 Shotwell St., San Francisco, CA   94110-1914
(415) 436-9333 • fax: (415) 436- 9993
e-mail: information@eff.org
website: www.eff.org

EFF is an organization that aims to promote better understanding of telecommunications issues. It fosters awareness of civil liberties issues arising from advancements in computer-based communications media and supports litigation to preserve, protect, and extend First Amendment rights in computing and telecommunications technologies. EFF's publications include *Building the Open Road, Crime and Puzzlement*, the quarterly newsletter *Networks & Policy*, the biweekly electronic newsletter *EFFector Online*, and white papers and articles, many of which are available on its website.

i-Safe, Inc.
6189 El Camino Real, Suite 201, Carlsbad, CA   92009
(760) 603-7911 • fax: (760) 603-8382
website: www.isafe.org

i-Safe is a nonprofit foundation dedicated to educating students on how to use the Internet safely, responsibly, and productively and how to avoid inappropriate and unlawful online content. It publishes online learning programs and provides educational services such as the i-LEARN Online program and the i-Mentor network, an "On Demand" learning experience.

National Center for Missing and Exploited Children (NCMEC)
Charles B. Wang International Children's Building
199 Prince St., Alexandria, VA   22314-3175
(703) 224-2150 • fax: (703) 224-2122
website: www.missingkids.com

Since 1984, NCMEC has been working to reduce the number of children who go missing each year by providing extensive information about children who are missing, assisting in all aspects of cases involving missing children, and providing training programs to professionals encountering instances of child abduction and exploitation. The NCMEC also operates a CyberTipline allowing individuals to report any behavior related to online child exploitation. NCMEC operates the online resources NetSmartz for children and NetSmartz411 for parents, providing information about Internet safety. The center has also published reports such as "Blog Beware" and "Online Victimization of Youth: Five Years Later."

Pew Internet and American Life Project
1615 L Street NW, Suite 700, Washington, DC   20036
(202) 419-4500 • fax: (202) 419-4505
website: www.pewinternet.org

The Pew Internet and American Life Project is an initiative of the Pew Research Center. The project explores the impact of the Internet on children, families, communities, the workplace, schools, health care, and civic/political life. Pew Internet provides data and analysis on Internet usage and its effects on American society. On its website the project provides access to articles and reports, including *Cyberbullying*, "Teens and Social Media," and "Teens and Mobile Phones."

Take a Stand, Lend a Hand, Stop Bullying Now!
5600 Fishers Lane, Rockville, MD   20858
(888) 275-4772
website: http://stopbullyingnow.hrsa.gov.

This Health Resources and Services Administration campaign provides information from various government agencies to educate children and adults about bullying, including cyber-bullying, and improve community prevention efforts. Links on the website provide kids, teens, young adults, parents, edu-cators, and the community with fact sheets and tools, includ-ing "Cyberbullying," which details what victims, parents, and schools can do to deal with cyberbullying.

WiredSafety
96 Linwood Plaza, #417, Ft. Lee, NJ   07024-3701
(201) 463-8663
e-mail: askparry@wiredsafety.org
website: www.wiredsafety.org

Operating online since 1995, WiredSafety is an Internet patrol organization that not only monitors the web for safety viola-tions but also provides education on all aspects of Internet safety. Volunteers worldwide offer their time and are the driv-ing force of the organization. The WiredSafety website pro-vides information categorized and specialized for parents, educators, law enforcement, and youth; additionally, the web-site explores topical issues such as social networks, cyberbully-ing, and cyberdating. Links to issue and age specific projects such as Teenangels, WiredKids, StopCyberbullying, and Inter-net Super Heroes are available on the website as well.

Bibliography

Books

Barbara Coloroso | *The Bully, the Bullied, and the Bystander.* New York: Harper Collins, 2003.

Sameer Hinduja and Justin W. Patchin | *Bullying Beyond the Schoolyard: Preventing and Responding to Cyberbullying.* Thousand Oaks, CA: Corwin. 2009.

Thomas A. Jacobs | *Teen Cyberbullying Investigated: Where Do Your Rights End and Consequences Begin?* Minneapolis, MN: Free Spirit, 2010.

Robin M. Kowalski, Susan P. Limber, and Patricia W. Agatston | *Cyber Bullying: Bullying in the Digital Age.* Hoboken, NJ: Blackwell, 2008.

Samuel C. McQuade, James P. Colt, and Nancy B.B. Meyer | *Cyber Bullying: Protecting Kids and Adults from Online Bullies.* Westport, CT: Praeger, 2009.

John Palfrey and Urs Gasser | *Born Digital: Understanding the First Generation of Digital Natives.* New York: Basic, 2008.

Shaheen Shariff | *Cyber-bullying: Issues and Solutions for the School, the Classroom and the Home.* New York: Routledge, 2008.

Shaheen Shariff   *Truths and Myths of Cyber-Bullying:*
and Andrew H.   *International Perspectives on*
Churchill, eds.   *Stakeholder Responsibility and*
                     Children's Safety. New York: Peter
                     Lang, 2010.

Daniel J. Solove   *The Future of Reputation: Gossip,*
                     Rumor, and Privacy on the Internet.
                     New Haven, CT: Yale University
                     Press, 2007.

Richard Joseph   *Internet Safety.* New York: H.W.
Stein, ed.   Wilson, 2009.

Nancy E. Willard   *Cyberbullying and Cyberthreats:*
                     Responding to the Challenge of Online
                     Social Aggression, Threats, and
                     Distress. Champaign, IL: Research
                     Press, 2007.

Nancy E. Willard   *Cyber-Safe Kids, Cyber-Savvy Teens:*
                     Helping Young People Learn to Use the
                     Internet Safely and Responsibly.
                     Hoboken, NJ: Wiley, 2007.

Periodicals and Internet Sources

Caralee Adams   "Cyber Bullying: How to Make It
                     Stop," *Instructor*, September/October
                     2010.

Emily Bazelon   "What Really Happened to Phoebe
                     Prince?" *Slate*, July 20, 2010.

Jessica Bennett   "From Lockers to Lockup,"
                     Newsweek, October 11, 2010.

Lauren Collins "Friend Game: Behind the Online
Hoax That Led to a Girl's Suicide,"
New Yorker, January 21, 2008.

Nancy Cook "The Booming Anti-Bullying
Industry," *Newsweek*, October 4,
2010.

Current Events "Your Space: Schools Struggle to
Find Ways to Curb Cyberbullying
without Violating Student Rights
(Debate)," October 25, 2010.

Corinne "Electronic Media, Violence, and
David-Ferdon Adolescents: An Emerging Public
and Marci Health Problem," *Journal of
Feldman Hertz Adolescent Health*, December, 2007.

Diane Diamond "Internet Anonymity: Unleashing
Our Inner Sociopath," *Huffington
Post*, October 13, 2010.

Bulent Dilmac "Values as a Predictor of
and Didem Cyber-bullying among Secondary
Aydogan School Students," *International
Journal of Social Sciences*, Summer
2010.

Karen Fanning "Cyberspace Bullies: Why Do So
Many Kids Turn to Cyberbullying?
How Can You Help Stop It?" *Junior
Scholastic*, November 9, 2009.

Megan Feldman "Why Are Nice, Normal Girls Getting
Bullied Online?" *Glamour*, March
2010.

Mark Gibbs "Digital Citizenship," *Network World*,
October 11, 2010.

Harvard Health Commentaries   "Cyberbullying," April 14, 2010.

Jan Hoffman   "Poisoned Web; Online Bullies Pull Schools into the Fray," *New York Times*, June 27, 2010.

Stacy Teiche Khadaroo   "Rutgers Student Death: Has Digital Age Made Students Callous?" *Christian Science Monitor*, October 1, 2010.

Stacy Teiche Khadaroo   "One-third of US Teens Are Victims of Cyberbullying," *Christian Science Monitor*, October 8, 2010.

Abbott Koloff   "States Push for Cyberbully Controls," *USA Today*, February 7, 2008.

Alison Virginia King   "Constitutionality of Cyberbullying Laws: Keeping the Online Playground Safe for Both Teens and Free Speech," *Vanderbilt Law Review*, April 2010.

Tamar Lewin   "Teenage Insults, Scrawled on Web, Not Walls," *New York Times*, May 5, 2010.

Lindsay McIntosh   "Children Facing New Torment As Bullies Move from the Playground to Cyberspace," *Times* [London], January 26, 2011.

Prevention Reader   "Remaining Safe and Avoiding Dangers Online: A Social Media Q & A with Kimberly Mitchell," December 2010.

PRWeb Newswire   "End Cyberbullying Now by Monitoring Internet Activity and Exposing Bullies," January 19, 2011.

Chris Riedel   "The Fight against Cyberbullying," *THE Journal [Technological Horizons in Education]*, May 2008.

Kirsten Scharnberg   "As Bullies Go Online, Schools Crack Down," *Chicago Tribune*, September 14, 2007.

John Schwartz   "Bullying, Suicide, Punishment," *New York Times*, October 2, 2010.

Pat Scales   "Preventing Cyberbullying: Who's Responsible for Teaching Kids How to Behave Online?" *School Library Journal*, January 2011.

Sara Stroud   "Fight Fire with Fire: School Districts Are Turning the Tables against Cyberbullies, Using Technology to Flush Out and Crack Down on Online Harassment," *THE Journal [Technological Horizons in Education]*, October 2009.

DeWayne Wickham   "Privacy No More? Tyler Clementi's Death Should Rattle Us All," *USA Today*, October 4, 2010.

Michael Yapko   "We're Too Proud of Our Anger," *Huffington Post*, October 7, 2010.

Index

A

Adolescent behavior, 7, 25
Aftab, Parry, 14
Alderman, Elizabeth, 66
Alexander, Ronald, 33
American Academy of Pediatrics (AAP), 64, 66
American Civil Liberties Union (ACLU), 11
Annenberg Program on Online Communities, 95
Anti-bullying programs, 26–27, 48, 51, 61, 79
Archives of General Psychiatry (journal), 49
Archives of Suicide Research (journal), 63
Australia, 94

B

Bates, Trinity, 94
Bauman, Sheri, 45
Bazelon, Emily, 8–9
Berkman Center for Internet and Society, 20
Beverly Vista School, 74
Billitteri, Thomas J., 10
Bligh, Ann, 94
Brunault, Brian, 14
Bullying, 23–27, 29, 39, 43–45
    cyberbullies, 15, 28, 40–41, 45, 48 50–51
    cyberbullying, 7–11, 15, 24, 30–31, 39, 55, 59, 60, 70
    cyberbullying as crime, 8–9, 11
    cyberbullying curricula, 43, 46
    cyberbullying punishment, 8, 10, 13, 46–47, 70
    school disciplinary policies, 10, 71–78
    school playground bullying, 58
    victims of bullying, 7–9, 30, 50–51, 55
Butler, Paul, 10

C

Centers for Disease Control and Prevention (CDC), 7, 26
Civil rights. *See* First Amendment rights
Civil Rights Act of 1964, 80, 86, 88
Clementi, Tyler, 7–11, 24, 29, 34, 80, 82
Cohen, Evan, 76
Columbine High School, 58
Common Sense Media, 42
Cox, John, 84
Creeley, Will, 83
Cyberbullies. *See* Bullying
Cyberbullying laws, 11, 16, 22, 86
Cyberbullying polling data, 10, 31, 57
Cyberbullying Research Center, 7, 40, 45, 52
Cybercrimes unit/specialists, 14, 21–22

K

Karnik, Niranjan, 62
Kouri, Jim, 57

L

Lautenberg, Frank, 80
Library of Congress, 44
Lukianoff, Greg, 80

M

Massachusetts General Hospital, 65
Megan Meier Cyberbullying Prevention Act, 85
Meier, Megan, 7–11, 24, 85, 88, 90, 95
Monitoring software, 19
Montefiore Medical Center, 66
Morris, John, 94
Moyer, Christine S., 62
Murphy, Wendy J., 67
MySpace, 7–9, 24, 35, 85, 95
See also Social networking and media

N

NAACP v. Claiborne Hardware (1982), 90
National Crime Preventaion Council, 64
Network World (journal), 89
New York City, 51
New York Times (newspaper), 32
North, Karen, 95

O

O'Keefe, Gwen Schurgin, 64
Online harassment, 10, 15, 61–65
Online identity impersonation, 13, 17, 21
Online rumors, 7, 24, 30, 54, 75
See also Bullying
Online supervision, 19

P

Parent-child relationships, 19–21, 59–61, 70
communication, 20–21
supervision, 55, 58–61
Patchin, Justin W., 7, 52, 88
Patient screening, 63
Pediatrics (journal), 65
Peer relationships, 30–31, 36, 39–40, 43, 51, 53–55, 60, 65
People (magazine), 29
Pew Research Center, 20, 64
Internet and American Life Project, 20, 54
Pollowitz, Greg, 85
Prince, Phoebe, 7–11, 29, 38–39, 45, 46, 49, 67–68, 70

Q

Quigley, Megan, 16

R

Ravi, Dharun, 7
Reiberg, Steven, 48
Ringwald, Molly, 29
Roberts-Pittman, Bridget, 58
Rutgers University, 7, 24, 34